Wisdom

OF THE

Proverbs

Explained

COLEMAN G. RECTOR

"My son, do not let wisdom and understanding out of your sight, preserve sound judgment and discretion;"

—*Proverbs 3:21*

© Copyright 2021 by Coleman G. Rector

All rights reserved. No part of this publication may be reproduced, stored in a retrieval system, or transmitted in any form or by any means—electronic, mechanical, photocopy, recording, or any other—except for brief quotations in printed reviews, without the prior permission from the author or publisher.

Scriptures are taken from THE HOLY BIBLE, NEW INTERNATIONAL VERSION®, NIV® Copyright © 1973, 1978, 1984, 2011 by Biblica, Inc.® Used by permission. All rights reserved worldwide.

Cover by Callie Rector

ISBN: 9798523101816

By Coleman G. Rector

TABLE OF CONTENTS

WISDOM OF THE PROVERBS EXPLAINED	5
PROVERBS 1	9
PROVERBS 2	19
PROVERBS 3	27
PROVERBS 4	39
PROVERBS 5	45
PROVERBS 6	51
PROVERBS 7	61
PROVERBS 8	67
PROVERBS 9	73
PROVERBS 10	77
PROVERBS 11	89
PROVERBS 12	105
PROVERBS 13	117
PROVERBS 14	131
PROVERBS 15	149
PROVERBS 16	167
PROVERBS 17	181
PROVERBS 18	193
PROVERBS 19	203
PROVERBS 20	215
PROVERBS 21	229
PROVERBS 22	241
PROVERBS 23	251
PROVERBS 24	261
PROVERBS 25	273

Proverbs 26	283
Proverbs 27	293
Proverbs 28	303
Proverbs 29	315
Proverbs 30	327
Proverbs 31	335
Bibliography	343

By Coleman G. Rector

WISDOM

OF THE PROVERBS EXPLAINED

Proverbs 3:21-22 says, "My son, do not let wisdom and understanding out of your sight, preserve sound judgement and discretion; they will be life for you, an ornament to grace your neck."

Wisdom, woven into the human fabric, is the desire to learn and understand. Knowledge, book learning, and facts are all great, but there is a vast difference between knowledge and wisdom. *Wisdom* means masterful understanding and skill. It is applying knowledge to real life. We may have knowledge, but without wisdom, our knowledge is wasted. We must learn to live out what we know.

Proverbs was written by King Solomon, the wisest man who ever lived, and several other wise individuals. King Solomon left a legacy of wisdom that are three books of the Bible: Proverbs, Ecclesiastes, and Song of Songs. In these books, under the inspiration of the Holy

Spirt, he gives practical insights and guidelines for life. This book will focus on trying to explain Proverbs in everyday terms, the way a parent would explain it to a child.

Proverbs is a collection of wise statements that offer hundreds of practical examples on how to live according to godly wisdom.

Proverbs has several audiences: 1) the young and simple getting ready to go out into the world, 2) the unwise trying to find wisdom, and 3) the wise who seek more wisdom. Proverbs covers a wide range of topics including youth and discipline; family life; self-control and resisting temptation; business matters; words and the tongue; knowing God; marriage; seeking the truth; wealth and poverty; honor; pride and arrogance; and, of course, wisdom. The Proverbs are riddles and parables outlining common-sensical life skills that youth have not yet experienced.

The purpose of this book is to make Proverbs less intimidating and more understandable. New readers sometimes get frustrated because they cannot understand the verbiage and parables and stop reading. My intention is to explain the proverbs in today's terminology so that everyone can read and understand them without feeling intimidated.

While the world has changed a lot since Proverbs was written in 700 BC, many things remain the same. Heed the experience and wisdom from these wise men. Learn from their mistakes and not your own, and you'll be many steps ahead in life because of it.

Every mother and father should read this book to their

children and grandchildren. And for those adults seeking wisdom but don't know how to find it, this book is a great place to start.

PROVERBS 1

PURPOSE AND THEME

1 The Proverbs of Solomon, Son of David, King of Israel;
2 For gaining wisdom and instruction;
   for understanding words of insight;
3 For receiving instruction in prudent behavior,
   doing what is right and just and fair;
4 for giving prudence to those who are simple,
   knowledge and discretion to the young—
5 let the wise listen and add to their learning,
   and let the discerning get guidance—
6 for understanding proverbs and parables,
   the sayings and riddles of the wise.

Proverbs 1:1-6 lay out the purpose and the goals of the book, which are to help followers of God gain wisdom and instruction, understand words of insight, receive instruction on prudent behavior, and do what is right and just and fair.

We all have an inherent knowledge of what is right and just and fair. We can feel it in our stomachs when we see someone being treated unfairly or unjustly.

We should go out of our way to do what is right, go out of our way to do what is just, and go out of our way to do what is fair. There is a lot more wisdom in the Proverbs, but this is a good introductory summation.

Other pieces of information are highlighted by:

- "…gaining wisdom and instruction…" (verse 2)
- "…understanding words of insight…" (verse 2)
- "…receiving instruction on prudent behavior…" (verse 3)
- "…let the wise listen and add to their learning…" (verse 5)
- "…let the discerning get guidance…" (verse 5)

These are all acts of learning for people who need wisdom. We must want to learn. We must want to receive the learning. We must be open to it.

> 7 The fear of the Lord is the beginning of knowledge, but fools despise wisdom and instruction.

Fearing the Lord means to honor and respect God, to live in awe of God's power, and to obey His Word. Fear and faith in God need to be the foundation and controlling principles in our lives, our understanding of the world, our attitudes, our speech, and our actions.

Verse 7 says "…but fools despise wisdom and instruction." A fool is a person who acts unwisely, imprudently, or silly. A fool is a know-it-all, a person who does not take the advice or the counsel of others smarter than himself or herself. A fool is a simpleton who is morally deficient and characterized by irrational behavior.

Fools believe they're the smartest people in the room, so they don't need to learn anything else. The truth is, they hate learning and instruction. Fools are so proud and arrogant to think they don't need to learn anything new because they already know everything.

We must keep learning if we are to avoid becoming fools. We don't stop learning just because we finish school. Learning means being open to change, open to new ideas, new ways of doing things, better ways of doing things, better ways of talking and acting. Learning is a lifelong game and is the key to gaining wisdom.

Not being a fool starts with "The fear of the Lord is the beginning of knowledge" because the fear of the Lord is the foundation of wisdom. It all starts with the fear, respect, and faith in the Lord. If we have a healthy fear of the Lord and an attitude that we want to keep learning, wisdom will fall into its place.

PROLOGUE
EXHORTATIONS TO EMBRACE WISDOM
WARNING AGAINST THE INVITATION OF SINFUL MEN

> 8 Listen, my son, to your father's instruction
> and do not forsake your mother's teaching.
> 9 They are a garland to grace your head
> and a chain to adorn your neck.

We should listen to the advice, instruction, and teaching of our fathers, mothers, grandfathers, and grandmothers, regardless of how old we are. They have been around a lot longer than we have, which usually means they have more wisdom than we do. Just as one displays a hat on his or her head or a gold chain around his or her neck, we should display our parents' teaching and instruction in all that we do. This shows the value and distinction of the wisdom we have gained.

> 10 My son, if sinful men entice you,
> do not give in to them.
> 11 If they say, "Come along with us;
> let's lie in wait for innocent blood,
> let's ambush some harmless soul;
> 12 let's swallow them alive, like the grave,
> and whole, like those who go down to the pit;
> 13 we get all sorts of valuable things
> and fill our houses with plunder;

14 cast lots with us;
   we will all share the loot"—
15 my son, do not go along with them,
   do not set foot on their paths;
16 for their feet rush to evil,
   they are swift to shed blood.

We should not be enticed by sinful men (or women), who promise easy money or goods. They will attack innocent people, steal from them, harm, or even kill them in the process. They will fill their houses with all the money and goods they have stolen and killed for and then invite us to share what they have. We must learn to make choices, not based on flashy appeal or short-range pleasures, but on what is just and right with long-term consequences considered.

Think of a path that forks. The crooked path goes off to the left and leads to wickedness, sin, death, and ruin, while the straight path leads to righteousness, wisdom, and prosperity. Stay on the straight path.

17 How useless to spread a net
   where every bird can see it!
18 These men lie in wait for their own blood;
   they ambush only themselves!
19 Such are the paths of all who go after ill-gotten gain;
   it takes away the life of those who get it.

Sin makes us feel we can get rich quick and be part of the crowd. Such people, however, are fools and will be caught in their own trap; they only ambush themselves! Maybe they get away with it once, twice, or even three times, but at the end of the day, they get caught or worse. Ever hear the saying, "live by the sword, die by the sword"? They will die at the hands of someone they attack to steal money and goods, the authorities, or possibly one of their own who doesn't want to share the plunder. Falling in with the wicked crowd and believing their enticing schemes is a path down the crooked road that leads to death and ruin.

WISDOM'S REBUKE

20 Out in the open wisdom calls aloud,
   she raises her voice in the public square;
21 on top of the wall she cries out,
   at the city gate she makes her speech:
22 "How long will you who are simple love your
   simple ways?

   How long will mockers delight in mockery
   and fools hate knowledge?

Wisdom is out there in plain sight, loud and clear. In this proverb, it is referred to as a woman, Lady Wisdom. We just have to be conscious of wisdom's availability and take advantage of it. How long will we love our "simple ways?" How long will we be mockers and fools who hate knowledge? We need to wake up and pay attention. Wisdom is out there. All we have to do is seek it and we shall find it. If we ask, we will receive. Wisdom is offered free of charge, so we should take advantage of it.

> 23 Repent at my rebuke!
>   Then I will pour out my thoughts to you,
>   I will make known to you my teachings.
> 24 But since you refuse to listen when I call
>   and no one pays attention when I stretch out my hand,
> 25 since you disregard all my advice
>   and do not accept my rebuke,
> 26 I in turn will laugh when disaster strikes you;
>   I will mock when calamity overtakes you—
> 27 When calamity overtakes you like a storm,
>   when disaster sweeps over you like a whirlwind,
>   when distress and trouble overwhelm you.

Refusing God's wisdom is a result of two things:

1) Being too proud, thinking more highly of our own wisdom and desires than of God's.
2) Being completely ignorant of wisdom at all, especially God's wisdom.

But if we repent at God's rebuke, He will pour out His thoughts and make His teachings known to us. God's thoughts! God's teachings! The holy grail of information.

The word *repent* means to feel or express sincere regret or remorse about wrongdoing or sin, and the word *rebuke* indicates a sharp disapproval or criticism of someone because of his or her behavior or actions.

So, God rebukes those who are mockers and fools who hate knowledge. And when He rebukes us, we should say we're sorry because we truly have feelings of regret. Then we need to stop being mockers and fools and humbly seek God's knowledge and wisdom.

Verse 24 says, "But since you refuse to listen when I call and no one pays attention when I stretch out my hand…." The saying "You can lead a horse to water, but you can't make him drink," comes to mind. You can lead a mocker and a fool to wisdom and understanding, but you can't make him or her listen or understand. God has stretched out His hand to us, but many have refused to listen. They pay no attention, disregard, God's advice, and refuse His rebuke. As a result, these people have refused the wisdom God offers to us freely. If this is true for you, then when disaster strikes and calamity overtakes you, God will laugh.

> 28 "Then they will call to me but I will not answer,
>   they will look for me but will not find me,
> 29 since they hated knowledge
>   and did not choose to fear the Lord.
> 30 Since they would not accept my advice
>   and spurned my rebuke,

> 31 they will eat the fruit of their ways
> and be filled with the fruit of their schemes.
> 32 For the waywardness of the simple will kill them,
> and the complacency of fools will destroy them;
> 33 but whoever listens to me will live in safety
> and be at ease, without fear of harm.

Those who choose to be mockers and fools who hate knowledge, those who refuse to listen or pay attention when God reaches out His hand, "will eat the fruit of their ways." In other words, they will fall victim to the very scheme they are planning because their attitudes and actions, their wayward ways, will kill them. If they choose not to accept knowledge, then their stupidity will catch up to them and ultimately destroy them.

All is not lost, however. These people can still repent at God's rebuke. They can still turn to Him and humble themselves, realizing they don't know everything. In fact, they don't know anything. They can still ask God for His knowledge when He reaches out His hand. Then they need to accept it, absorb it, and live it. Daily prayers asking God for strength, guidance, and wisdom will help facilitate this.

Proverbs 2

MORAL BENEFITS OF WISDOM

1. My son, if you accept my words
   and store up my commands within you,
2. turning your ear to wisdom
   and applying your heart to understanding—
3. indeed, if you call out for insight
   and cry aloud for understanding,
4. and if you look for it as for silver
   and search for it as for hidden treasure,
5. then you will understand the fear of the Lord
   and find the knowledge of God.

If we accept God's words, actively seek wisdom, cry aloud for understanding, and search for it as we would search for silver or hidden treasure, then we will understand the fear of the Lord and find the knowledge of God. We have to want it and we have to go after it like we're hunting for hidden treasure. If we do, we'll find it. For wisdom is far more valuable than silver or hidden treasure.

> 6 For the Lord gives wisdom;
>   from his mouth come knowledge and understanding.
> 7 He holds success in store for the upright,
>   he is a shield to those whose walk is blameless,
> 8 for he guards the course of the just
>   and protects the way of his faithful ones.

If we fear the Lord, and open our hearts to receive wisdom and understanding, He will give it to us. If we live upright lives, the Lord has success in store for us. If we walk blamelessly, the Lord will shield us. If we live just and faithful lives to the Lord, He will guard us and protect us.

> 9 Then you will understand what is right and just
>   and fair – and every good path.
> 10 For wisdom will enter your heart,
>   and knowledge will be pleasant to your soul.
> 11 Discretion will protect you,
>   and understanding will guard you.

If we choose to receive wisdom, we will understand what is right and just and fair. We will be able to recognize and choose the straight paths instead of the crooked paths. Wisdom will get into our hearts and souls to protect and guard us.

Disasters don't typically happen all by themselves.

They are usually a series of bad choices and crooked paths that compound on each other to cause the disaster. If, for example, you start hanging out with a bad crowd at school (mistake #1), your grades will suffer (mistake #2), and you'll care less and less about school and responsibilities (mistake #3). Then you'll get kicked off your sports team because you have bad grades and a bad attitude (mistake #4). Then you might start drinking and doing drugs (mistake #5) and go riding around with your new friends (mistake #6). You get pulled over by the police (mistake #7), and upon a search of the vehicle, the police find illegal drugs and guns that you had no idea were even in the car (mistake #8). Finally you get arrested and convicted on a felony charge and go to jail (mistake #9). While you're in jail, you find yourself in the middle of a turf/gang war and get beaten up and killed because you were at the wrong place at the wrong time with the wrong skin color (mistake #10).

So, you're dead, filled with the fruit of your schemes. Let's see how it happened. Did hanging out with a bad crowd kill you? No, but that was the root of the problem, your first crooked path. Did your suffering grades and change in attitude toward school kill you? No, but that was the next little mistake and crooked path. You got kicked off your sports team. Did that kill you? No, but your afternoons became free for drinking and doing drugs. Did that kill you? No, but again, another not-so-little mistake and another crooked path. Once you went cruising with your buddies and got arrested, the police, the judge, and the prison guards decided the rest of your life, that is, until you were killed in a prison war.

But if we seek and find wisdom, we'll be able to discern the right path from the crooked path and make good decisions. You see, good decisions compound into blessings. For example, you associate with a group of smart, good, and faithful kids at school (good choice #1). Your grades will also be good and you'll be successful in school because you'll have a good attitude (good choice #2). You will excel on your sports team because you practice a lot and try hard to be the best player you can be (good choice #3). And because you practice with your sports team every afternoon, you don't have lots of free time at home alone to make mistakes or go down crooked paths (good choice #4). So, instead of drinking and doing drugs, you decide to take some AP classes and join the engineering club (good choice #5).

As a result of all your good choices, you graduate in the top 5 percent of your class (blessing #1). You apply to six colleges and get accepted to five of them. As a result you are able to attend a great university (blessing #2). While you're in college, you study hard, play a sport, and get a business degree, graduating in the top 5 percent of your class (blessing #3). You accept a job with a fast track to advancement, making $100,000/ year (blessing #4). Then you meet the girl/guy of your dreams and decide to get married and start a family. As a result, you have a beautiful spouse, beautiful kids, and lots of fun vacations and family time (blessing #5). After five years at your job, you decide to start your own business (blessing #6).

Now, you have a big house on twenty-five acres, with a finished basement, and a pool (blessing #7). So after 10 years of running and growing your business, you accept an offer from your biggest competitor to sell your business to them for $25,000,000 and retire (blessing #8). Finally, you spend that last thirty years of your life enjoying your family, traveling, and establishing a foundation/charity for your favorite cause (blessing #9).

So, which path would you prefer to walk on?

12 Wisdom will save you from the ways of wicked men,
    from men whose words are perverse,
13 who have left the straight paths
    to walk in dark ways,
14 who delight in doing wrong
    and rejoice in the perverseness of evil,
15 whose paths are crooked
    and who are devious in their ways.

The word *perverse* (verse 12) means to be directed away from what is right and good. There are wicked people everywhere. They walk the crooked paths in the darkness, doing wrong things, and rejoicing in their perverseness of evil, all of which lead to death and ruin.

Wisdom will give us the knowledge and judgment to stay far away from these wicked people and not to associate with them in any way. This will ensure we will not take on any of their wicked ways.

> 16 Wisdom will save you also from the adulterous woman,
>   from the wayward woman and her seductive words,
> 17 who has left the partner of her youth
>   and ignored the covenant she made before God.
> 18 Surely her house leads down to death
>   and her paths to the spirits of the dead.
> 19 None who go to her return
>   or attain the paths of life.

Two of the most difficult sins to resist are pride and sexual immorality. Both are seductive. Pride says, "I deserve it"; sexual immorality says, "I need it." To make their appeal even more deadly, these two often work together. Only by relying on God's strength can we overcome them. As we continue to read the Proverbs we see they talk a lot about adultery, which is voluntary sexual intercourse between a married person and a person who is not his or her spouse. Adultery may look enticing at the time, but it can, and often does, destroy lives.

In the case of this proverb, a woman is trying to cheat on her husband with another man, and she is seducing him "with her seductive words." If you are the man who is having sex with another man's wife, possibly in their family home, and you succumb to the seductive words of the adulteress, you will discover that "Surely her house leads to death and her paths to the spirits of the dead" (verse 18) and that "None who go to her return or attain the paths of life." (verse 19)

If the jealous husband finds out about the affair, he could track you down and kill you, and your life would end there. Or, assuming you are married also, your wife may find out you've been sleeping with another woman and divorce you. As a result, you've destroyed your entire family for what may have been a cheap fifteen-minute thrill. You may even lose your job, due to the character flaws you've demonstrated, and your home.

Your wife will hate you because you've betrayed her. Your children will hate you for cheating on their mother and lying about it. You'll have to sell the house, and most of your wealth will be forfeited through alimony and child support. And the adulteress you fell head over heels for, who caused you to go down this crooked path… she's on to her next victim.

In the end, you're broke, you've lost your job, and you're alone because the people you love the most in the world will never want to see you or talk to you again. You're forty-five years old and have to start over as a person branded a loser.

Having wisdom will save you from choosing this crooked path that leads to death and ruin. Find wisdom!

> 20 Thus you will walk in the ways of the good
>   and keep the paths of the righteous.
> 21 For the upright will live in the land,
>   and the blameless will remain in it;
> 22 but the wicked will be cut off from the land,
>   and the unfaithful will be torn from it.

If we abide by the wisdom God has given us, we will walk in the ways of the good. We will follow the same paths the righteous people take. If we do this, we can stay in the land that God has given us. Or, we can be wicked and unfaithful and be cut off from the land, which means we would be dead.

PROVERBS 3

WISDOM BESTOWS WELL-BEING

1 My son do not forget my teaching,
   But keep my commands in your heart,
2 for they will prolong your life many years
   and bring you peace and prosperity.

Don't forget God's teaching and wisdom. Keeping His commands in our hearts means keeping them with us; making them part of who we are; and, most importantly, following God's teaching and wisdom. The heart is the essence of one's self, one's life. If we follow God's teaching and God's wisdom, they will prolong our lives many years. They will keep us out of trouble so we don't get killed doing something unwise, and they will bring us a life of peace, prosperity, health, and abundance.

> 3 Let Love and faithfulness never leave you;
>   bind them around your neck,
>   write them on the tablet of your heart.
> 4 Then you will win favor and a good name
>   in the sight of God and man.

Love and faithfulness are two amazing qualities we should keep with us always; we need to be openly loving and openly faithful to our families and those around us. Binding these qualities around our necks means displaying them like a necklace for all to see. Writing them on the tablets of our hearts is a permanent mark on our hearts and souls. It means making love and faithfulness part of our fabric, part of our being, part of who we are forever.

If we make them part of who we are, we will win favor and a good name in the sight of God and man. This means we will have a good name in God's eyes and a good name in the eyes of the public.

> 5 Trust in the Lord with all your heart
>   and lean not on your own understanding;
> 6 in all your ways submit to him,
>   and he will make your paths straight.

Proverbs 3:5-6 is one of the most quoted and memorized verses in the Bible. Why? Because it does a very good job of summarizing God's desired relationship with His people. The first word says it all, "Trust."

Another word used throughout the Bible is "faith."

God wants His people to put "all," not some, not most, all 100 percent of their faith in Him, all their trust in Him. That's what it means to trust in the Lord with all our hearts. It means with everything we have. Leaning not on our own understanding means not relying on what we think is right or wrong or what we think the outcome should be. It means not thinking we know more than God. We need to remember it's the Lord who has control.

Submitting to Him in all our ways means trusting Him completely, to turn whatever situation we're facing over to God in prayer. We need to ask God for strength, guidance, and wisdom to make right decisions. And if we do all these things, He will make our paths straight. Crooked paths lead to death and ruin. Trusting in the Lord will keep us on the straight paths. Trust God as if everything depends on Him, while working as if everything depends on you.

We are not to put ourselves in dangerous situations and hope that God will bail us out. That is another crooked path. We don't need to sit in the middle of a highway and hope a truck doesn't hit us. We must use our God-given talents and knowledge to function in a safe and healthy manner.

God's answers will come in various ways. He might speak to us in a dream. A stranger; a long, lost friend; or a distant relative may show up and offer us an opportunity. Or, sometimes, what is perceived as a bad event turns out to be a blessing. When one door shuts, God is always opening a new one. We might break up with a long-term significant other, but we'll meet the true love of our lives a month later on a blind date. There are countless stories of tragedies and horrific events that have happened to people, only to be turned into something life changing.

> 7 Do not be wise in your own eyes;
>   fear the Lord and shun evil.
> 8 This will bring health to your body
>   and nourishment to your bones.

To be wise in our own eyes is to be arrogant and egocentric. This often leads us down the crooked path that can only end in death and ruin. The fear of the Lord is the beginning of knowledge and the foundation of wisdom. Humbly fearing the Lord will help us shun evil and keep us on the straight path, which leads to righteousness, justice, prosperity, and health.

> 9 Honor the Lord with your wealth,
>   with the firstfruits of all your crops;
> 10 then your barns will be filled to overflowing,
>   and your vats will brim over with new wine.

The Bible calls for believers to give back to the Lord some of the wealth He has given us. This is called *tithing*. Tithing is normally considered to be 10 percent of our income to be given to honor the Lord. Most perceive this as giving money to our churches so it can be used to help people. One can also give money directly to help the poor, the sick, and the underprivileged through a foundation, a shelter, or a food bank.

Giving with the firstfruits of all our crops means we are to give the best of our income to the Lord, early, and not give merely what is left over at the end of the year. This establishes a trust in the Lord that He will provide for us.

If we tithe our firstfruits to the Lord, our barns will be filled to overflowing, and our vats will brim over with new wine, which means the Lord will provide for us in abundance.

> 11 My son, do not despise the Lord's discipline,
>   and do not resent his rebuke,
> 12 because the lord disciplines those he loves,
>   as a father the son he delights in.

The Lord's discipline is a form of instruction. This is the Lord taking interest in us, molding and shaping us, and making us fit to receive His rewards. Receiving His rebuke and not resenting it means that we love that God is bringing us back to the straight path. He's forging us into the people He wants us to be.

> 13 Blessed are those who find wisdom,
>   those who gain understanding,
> 14 for she is more profitable than silver
>   and yields better returns than gold.

> 15 She is more precious than rubies;
>   nothing you desire can compare with her.
> 16 Long life is in her right hand;
>   in her left hand are riches and honor.
> 17 Her ways are pleasant ways,
>   and all her paths are peace.
> 18 She is a tree of life to those who take hold of her;
>   those who hold her fast will be blessed.

This proverb refers to Lady Wisdom as "she." Those who find her have already found the fear of the Lord. They will be blessed with the long life, the riches, and the honor that she gives. Her ways are pleasant ways, and all her paths are peace.

The tree of life in verse 18 is a metaphor of delight and refreshment that ensures eternal life. If we hold on tight to Lady Wisdom, we will be blessed.

> 19 By wisdom the Lord laid the earth's foundations,
>   by understanding he set the heavens in place;
> 20 by his knowledge the watery depths were divided,
>   and the clouds let drop the dew.

Wisdom, understanding, and knowledge. This is how the Lord laid order to the earth, the heavens, and everything He created. These principles are built into all He created, which includes you, your life, and everything and everyone in it.

21 My son, do not let wisdom and understanding out of your sight,
Preserve sound judgement and discretion;
22 they will be life for you,
an ornament of grace around your neck.
23 Then you will go on your way in safety,
and your foot will not stumble.
24 When you lie down, you will not be afraid;
when you lie down, your sleep will be sweet.
25 Have no fear of sudden disaster
or the ruin that overtakes the wicked,
26 for the Lord will be at your side
and will keep your foot from being snared.

Wisdom, understanding, sound judgment, and discretion will be life for us. *Discretion* is the God-given ability to think and make good choices. *Sound judgment* includes not only discretion, but also knowledge that comes from instruction, training, and discipline, as well as the insight that results from knowing and applying God's teachings.

All these qualities will keep us on the straight path that leads to life, peace, prosperity, love, faithfulness, a good name, health, nourishment, riches, and honor, and away from the crooked path that leads to death and ruin.

As we saw earlier, we are to display wisdom, understanding, sound judgment, and discretion around our necks like an ornament (necklace) of grace for all to see. In this way, we share it with others so they might also seek wisdom. The Lord will be at our side to protect us, keep us from stumbling or being ensnared. He will be with us when we lie down so that our sleep will be peaceful and sweet.

> 27 Do not withhold good from those to whom it is due,
>   when it is in your power to act.
> 28 Do not say to your neighbor,
>   "come back tomorrow and I'll give it to you"—
>   when you already have it with you.

If we can help someone and we have the opportunity to do so, we should do it right away. Delaying help will create a barrier between us and the one looking for help. Telling the person, "Come back tomorrow and I'll see what I can do" means we think we're above the one God wants us to help. This is not how God wants us to act.

> 29 Do not plot harm against your neighbor,
>   who lives trustfully near you.
> 30 Do not accuse anyone for no reason—
>   when they have done you no harm.

Plotting harm against our neighbor will come back to haunt us because we will eventually be found out. Exodus 20 contains the ten commandments, which we must follow if we are to gain wisdom. The ninth commandment states "You shall not give false testimony against your neighbor." Accusing someone of doing something he or she didn't do, which makes that person subject to the law and penalty, is just plain evil and wrong.

While the ten commandments are not listed in Proverbs, several of them are referenced. They are as follows:

1) You shall have no other gods before me.
2) You shall not make for yourself an image in the form of anything in heaven above or on the earth beneath or in the waters below. You shall not bow down to them or worship them; for I, the Lord your God, am a jealous God, punishing the children for the sin of the parents to the third and fourth generation of those who hate me, but showing love to a thousand generations of those who love me and keep my commands.
3) You shall not misuse the name of the Lord your God, for the Lord will not hold anyone guiltless who misuses his name.
4) Remember the sabbath day by keeping it holy. Six days you shall labor and do all your work, but the seventh day is a sabbath to the Lord your God. On it you shall not do any work, neither you, nor your son or daughter, nor your male or female servant, nor your animals, nor any foreigner residing in your towns. For in six days the Lord made the heavens and the earth, the sea, and all that is in them, but he rested on the seventh day. Therefore the Lord blessed the sabbath day and made it holy.

5) Honor your father and your mother, so that you may live long in the land of the Lord your God is giving you.
6) You shall not murder.
7) You shall not commit adultery.
8) You shall not steal.
9) You shall not give false testimony against your neighbor.
10) You shall not covet your neighbor's house. You shall not covet your neighbor's wife, nor his male or female servant, his ox or donkey, or anything that belongs to your neighbor.

31 Do not envy the violent
or choose any of their ways.
32 For the Lord detests the perverse
but takes the upright into his confidence.
33 The Lords curse is on the house of the wicked,
but he blesses the home of the righteous.

We must not choose to be like or follow violent, perverse, or wicked people because the Lord detests these people and their ways. Being upright, good, and righteous in our actions and our ways will cause the Lord to take us into His confidence and bless our homes.

34 He mocks proud mockers
   but shows favor to the humble and oppressed.
35 The wise inherit honor,
   but fools only get shame.

A *mocker* is a person who jeers or treats something or someone poorly or with contempt. Basically this person is a loudmouth who has something negative to say about everyone and everything.

A *proud mocker* is an arrogant person who does the same thing. Proverbs 8:13 says the Lord hates pride and arrogance. A proud mocker, which is a terrible combination, is mocked by the Lord. The humble and the oppressed, on the other hand, will see favor in the eyes of the Lord. People who have wisdom will also have honor, but the foolish—those who act in wicked, perverse, and violent ways—will receive only shame.

PROVERBS 4

GET WISDOM AT ANY COST

1 Listen my son to a father's instruction;
   pay attention and gain understanding.
2 I give you sound learning,
   so do not forsake my teaching.
3 For I too was a son to my father,
   still tender, and cherished by my mother.
4 Then he taught me, and he said to me,
   "Take hold of my words with all your heart;
   keep my commands and you will live.
5 Get wisdom, get understanding;
   do not forget my words or turn away from them.
6 Do not forsake wisdom, and she will protect you;
   love her, and she will watch over you.
7 The beginning of wisdom is this: Get wisdom.
   Though it cost all you have, get understanding.

8 Cherish her, and she will exalt you;
   embrace her, and she will honor you.
9 She will give you a garland to grace your head
   and present you with a glorious crown.

This is a father, in this case, King Solomon, telling his son how his father, David, instructed him in wisdom and understanding as a young boy. It is a parent's responsibility to pass on wisdom and understanding to the next generation. If our parents did not pass it on to us, then we must begin the cycle of learning and understanding. Reading and studying the book of Proverbs is a good way to gain it.

God, our Father, wants us as His children to take His words into our hearts and make them part of who we are, so we need to ask Him for wisdom and understanding daily. Once we gain it, we are to love her and she will watch over us. Lady Wisdom will protect and exalt us because she teaches us how to live and how to stay off the crooked path that leads to death and ruin. Wisdom and understanding will serve us well and give us life and prosperity.

10 Listen, my son, accept what I say,
   and the years of your life will be many.
11 I instruct you in the way of wisdom
   And lead you along straight paths.
12 When you walk, your steps will not be hampered;
   when you run, you will not stumble.

Proverbs 4 41

13 Hold on to instruction, do not let it go;
   guard it well, for it is your life.
14 Do not set foot on the path of the wicked
   or walk in the way of evildoers.
15 Avoid it, do not travel on it;
   turn from it and go on your way.
16 For they cannot rest until they do evil,
   they are robbed of sleep till they make someone stumble.
17 They eat the bread of wickedness
   and drink the wine of violence.

The straight path leads to a long life, riches, honor, pleasant ways, and paths of peace. The crooked path leads to wickedness, violence, and death. Those who have wisdom and understanding know to keep on the straight path and not set foot on the crooked path. If we find ourselves on a crooked path, we are to turn from it and go on our way.

Evil people are good at persuading unwise people to follow them. So, we may go down a path, thinking it's a straight path when suddenly the person we are with or that we are listening to tells us that he or she is an evil person with wicked intentions. That's when we should get out of that situation by saying something like:

- "My mom is calling me."
- "I'm late for dinner."
- "It's past curfew, and I have to go home."
- "I love my wife [or husband] and my family."
- "This violates my probation."

Whatever we need to come up with, we should come up with it and get out of there and back on the straight path. Evil people thrive on being evil and wicked. We are not to associate with them.

If your best friend has started to do evil and wicked things and is trying to persuade you to do the same, divorce your friend and your friendship. This person will drag you into their quagmire of wickedness. Best friends can talk you into doing things you know you shouldn't do: drugs, alcohol, stealing… "C'mon, nobody's going to find out. It's cool." You know better than that. Find a set of friends who fear the Lord and walk-in faith with God and walk with them instead.

> 18 The path of the righteous is like the morning sun,
>   shining ever brighter till the full light of day.
> 19 But the way of the wicked is like deep darkness;
>   they do not know what makes them stumble.
> 20 My son, pay attention to what I say;
>   turn your ear to my words.
> 21 Do not let them out of your sight,
>   keep them within your heart;
> 22 for they are life to those who find them
>   and health for one's whole body.
> 23 Above all else, guard your heart,
>   for everything you do flows from it.
> 24 Keep your mouth from perversity;
>   keep corrupt talk far from your lips.

> 25 Let your eyes look straight ahead;
> fix your gaze directly before you.
> 26 Give careful thought to the paths for your feet
> and be steadfast in all your ways.
> 27 Do not turn to the right or left,
> keep your foot from evil.

The wicked don't have the light of wisdom to guide their way. They do not see the consequences of their actions, so they fall. Once again, as is so often repeated in the book of Proverbs, we need to guard our hearts. To a great extent, our feelings of love and desire dictate how we live because we focus on the things we enjoy. So those feelings and desires need to lead us down the straight path.

Greed, for example, will lead us down a crooked path because having an overwhelming desire to accumulate wealth makes us do bad things. Lust will also lead us down a crooked path. By contrast, a loving relationship with a good person will build a good family. An education will lead to a good job or starting a business. Practicing our faith in God and participating in our churches will grow our relationship with Him. Helping people or being a coach or a volunteer are also good ways to be an encouragement to others.

Everything we do flows from what's in our hearts; it's who we are. It's our character, our being. That's why it's important we keep God's words in our hearts (verse 21). If we have hearts full of evil, greed, and lust, these character flaws will show themselves in actions and words.

We need to have hearts filled with wisdom, understanding, love, and grace so that those qualities will flow from us. Keeping our mouths free from nasty talk and manipulative words and lies will help keep our hearts from becoming corrupt as well, leaving only good things to flow out of us.

Keeping our eyes straight ahead means staying on the straight path. The evil people and things are off to the side, and we need to avoid eye contact with them so we don't give them a chance to infect us. Being steadfast in all our ways and staying on the straight path will serve us well.

PROVERBS 5

WARNING AGAINST ADULTERY

1 My son, pay attention to my wisdom,
   turn your ear to my words of insight,
2 that you may maintain discretion
   and your lips may preserve knowledge.
3 For the lips of the adulterous woman drip honey,
   and her speech is smoother than oil;
4 but in the end she is bitter as gall,
   sharp as the double-edged sword.
5 Her feet go down to death;
   her steps lead straight to the grave.
6 She gives no thought to the way of life;
   her paths wander aimlessly, but she does not know it.

Once again the adulteress is raised because this is one of the easiest ways to go down a crooked path and end up dead. I addressed this in detail in Proverb 2:16-19, so please refer back to that commentary. Also, while the father instructs his son in verse 5:1 to "pay attention to my wisdom," the adulterous man needs to do the same.

This proverb, however, refers to a woman cheating with another man, trying to seduce him "with her speech smoother than oil." What starts out as the taste of honey on her lips ends in the bitter taste of gall. In the end, she leads the man "straight into the grave" because she doesn't even care about her own life, so she surely won't care about his.

Having wisdom will save us from choosing this crooked path that leads to death and ruin.

> 7 Now then, my sons, listen to me;
>   do not turn aside from what I say.
> 8 Keep to a path far from her,
>   do not go near the door of her house,
> 9 lest you lose your honor to others
>   and your dignity to one who is cruel,
> 10 lest strangers feast on your wealth
>   and your toil enrich the house of another.
> 11 At the end of your life you will groan,
>   when your flesh and body are spent.
> 12 You will say, "How I hated discipline!
>   How my heart spurned correction!
> 13 I would not obey my teachers
>   or turn my ear to my instructors.
> 14 And I was soon in serious trouble
>   in the assembly of God's people."

The father urges the son once again not to ignore what he is teaching him, which in this case, is to stay away from the adulterous woman and her house, or wherever she resides. It's going to get out; it always does. And when it does, honorable and wise people will look down on you because you commit dishonorable acts. And strangers will feast on your wealth and your hard work to add to their own homes.

There will almost always be a divorce. And when that happens, the home, bank accounts, stocks, bonds, and other assets are divided, regardless of whose name is on them because they will all be considered marital assets. The judge will require the one who committed the adultery to come up with a settlement for his or her spouse, and most of the time it must be in cash. There will be a timeline set; if the adulterer fails to comply with the timeline, he or she can be held in contempt of court and put in jail and then the court will sell off the assets.

Selling the assets for a good price is "if-y" since everyone will know you're being raked over the coals by your angry spouse, his or her top-notch divorce lawyer (who the adulterer will have to pay for), and a judge who is not impressed by dishonorable actions. Consequently, any assets will sell for a fraction of what they are worth to the nearest bottom-fisher who has cash. Strangers feasting on your wealth that you obtained from your life's hard work will now enrich the house of another.

When all is said and done, the adulterer is hated, dishonored, broke, and completely at a loss of how it all happened. If he or she would have only listened to his or her dad's wisdom, not hated discipline and spurred correction, he or she could have avoided being in serious trouble in the assembly of God's people—the court system.

> 15 Drink water from your own cistern,
> Running water from your own well.

This is referring to a spouse and the fact that he or she should make love with his or her spouse, not with someone else's.

> 16 Should your springs overflow in the streets,
> Your streams of water in the public square?
> 17 Let them be yours alone,
> Never to be shared with strangers.

A spouse should also never share his or her spouse with another. It's adultery, and we've just seen the consequences of that. Even if it's consensual, it will be a burden on a spouse's relationship for the rest of his or her life and may cause the end of it.

> 18 May your fountain be blessed,
> and may you rejoice in the wife of your youth.
> 19 A loving doe, a graceful deer__
> may her breasts satisfy you always,
> may you ever be intoxicated with her love.

Those who are married should enjoy their spouses forever and never divorce them to find someone younger or "better." The spouses they should enjoy are the ones they married in their youth, the ones they swore before God to love, honor, and be there for in sickness and in health. They should be intoxicated with one another's love and their bodies.

> 20 Why, my son, be intoxicated with another man's wife?
> Why embrace the bosom of a wayward woman?
> 21 For your ways are in full view of the Lord,
> and he examines all your paths.
> 22 The evil deeds of the wicked ensnare them;
> the cords of their sins hold them fast.
> 23 For lack of discipline they will die,
> led astray by their own great folly.

Spouses need to be happy with one another, their families, and their relationship. Committing adultery is wicked and evil, and those who do this are wayward. The Lord is in full view of everyone's actions; He examines whether we're going down the straight path or the crooked path.

The evil deeds of the wicked, especially adultery, always return to haunt them. They will be ensnared in their wickedness and their sin and pay the price of death for their lack of discipline—for taking the crooked path and being led astray by their own great folly.

Proverbs 6

Warnings Against Folly

1 My son, if you have put up security for your neighbor,
   if you have shaken hands in pledge for a stranger,
2 you have been trapped by what you said,
   ensnared by the words of your mouth.
3 So do this, my son, to free yourself,
   since you have fallen into your neighbor's hands:
   Go—to the point of exhaustion—
   and give your neighbor no rest!
4 Allow no sleep to your eyes,
   no slumber to your eyelids.
5 Free yourself, like a gazelle from the hand of the hunter,
   like a bird from the snare of the fowler.

This proverb is about agreeing to take the responsibility of another person's, or your neighbor's debt. Putting up security means giving something of yours, or agreeing to give something of yours, to a lender if your neighbor does not pay the debt.

If you shake your neighbor's hand and tell him or her that you'll take the responsibility of your neighbor's debt if he or she does not pay it, that is a binding pledge, and you and your family are obligated. In that event, "you have been trapped by what you said, ensnared by the words of your mouth."

Words have consequences. By saying you will take responsibility for your neighbor's debt, you have now removed the burden from your neighbor and put it onto yourself and your family. This is equivalent to co-signing a loan. You are now trapped with the debt and your neighbor can do whatever he or she wants. That person may choose not to pay back the debt because the responsibility has now been shifted to you.

If you can't pay it back, the lender can take everything you and your family have—your money, your home, and your possessions. During the time Proverbs was written, someone who owed a debt could be forced into slavery in order to satisfy it.

So, consider wisely any decision to take on another person's debt. You may just want to help a neighbor out, but consider the consequences. It's amazing how people's attitudes shift once they have shifted the burden of debt to someone else. They will miss a payment and come to you for help, all the while you'll notice the new gold rings on their hand and the new car they are driving. But you still have to help them make good on the debt anyway because your name is attached to it.

Proverbs 6

The loan will eventually go into default, and the lender will come to you for the repayment of the entire debt. Once they get a judgment against you, they will start cleaning out your savings account and foreclose on your house and any other properties you may own.

When you go after your neighbor, you'll discover he or she is nowhere to be found. So, how do you get out of this mess?

You harass your neighbor or friend, day and night, until he or she lets you off your obligation, or most likely pays off the debt. Until that happens, however, you ensure your neighbor doesn't get a minute's rest.

In today's world, if you cosign a legal note with a lender, there is no getting out of it. You have two options: 1) Have your neighbor get a new loan that you did not cosign to pay, or 2) Harass, guilt, and shame your neighbor until he or she pays off the debt. Most cosigned loans are paid by the cosigner. Don't fall into that trap.

6 Go to the ant, you sluggard;
 consider its ways and be wise!
7 It has no commander,
 no overseer or ruler,
8 yet it stores its provisions in summer
 and gathers its food at harvest.
9 How long will you lie there, you sluggard?
 When will you get up from your sleep?
10 A little sleep, a little slumber,
 a little folding of the hands to rest—

11 and poverty will come on you like a thief
and scarcity like an armed man.

We've all seen ants crawling all over the place, carrying food bigger than they are, back to the ant hill. They work with prudence and diligence and rarely stop. A sluggard, on the other hand, is a person who demonstrates laziness and a poor work ethic. Those who are sluggards need to watch the ants and learn from their example. The ant has no one standing over it, no overseer, yet it still works tirelessly gathering food. That is the work ethic that sluggards need to replicate.

As wonderful as sleep is, and as much as everyone loves it, there is a time for sleep and a time for work. While it is necessary to sleep every day, the sabbath is the day to catch up on our rest. Being lazy or being home sleeping while we should be working will cause poverty to come on us like a thief, which means it will happen so fast we won't see it coming. Poverty and scarcity rob us of the legitimate rest we should enjoy.

Having a good work ethic is part of being wise. People who have a good work ethic work hard, make money, and provides for themselves and their families. Sluggards do not work, take no responsibility for it, and rely on others or the government to take care of them. They let themselves and their families down. Laziness often leads to desperation and a trip down a crooked path for fast rewards with ill-gotten gains.

Proverbs 6

> 12 A troublemaker and a villain,
>   who goes about with a corrupt mouth,
> 13 who winks maliciously with his eye,
>   signals with his feet
>   and motions with his fingers,
> 14 who plots evil with deceit in his heart—
>   he always stirs up conflict.
> 15 Therefore disaster will overtake him in an instant;
>   he will suddenly be destroyed – without remedy.

Troublemakers and villains agitate against all that is right. They constantly say things to stir up controversy. They'll wink at you suggestively, motion with their fingers, and say, "Hey, come here. I want to talk to you."

But then, divine justice will strike, and the troublemaker/villain will suddenly be destroyed without remedy. Recall Proverbs 1:31-32: "they will eat the fruit of their ways and be filled with the fruit of their schemes."

> 16 There are six things the Lord hates,
>   seven that are detestable to him:
> 17 haughty eyes,
>   a lying tongue,
>   hands that shed innocent blood,
> 18 a heart that devises wicked schemes,
>   feet that are quick to rush to evil,
> 19 a false witness who pours out lies
>   and a person who stirs up conflict in the community.

The Lord hates these six or seven things:
1) Haughty Eyes – People who display an arrogant demeanor and attitude, setting themselves above others. Scripture says repeatedly that God is resistant to haughtiness. In fact, He brings down the haughty and the proud.
2) A Lying Tongue – People who tell lies. People who knowingly and willingly deceive others.
3) Hands that Shed Innocent Blood – People who hurt and kill innocent people for any reason.
4) A Heart that Devises Wicked Schemes – People who conceive evil against others, for personal reasons or for misguided objectives like terrorism or politics.
5) Feet that are Quick to Rush to Evil – People who have no resistance to doing what is wrong. They are quick to rush into evil plans or schemes.
6) A False Witness Who Pours Out Lies – This is similar to #2, the lying tongue; however, this is worse than just telling a lie. This is telling a lie with the intent of sending an innocent person to prison or to his or her death. This is also the ninth commandment of God's law.
7) A Person Who Stirs Up Conflict in the Community – Opposite of being a peacemaker, this is a person who purposely disrupts the peace in the community, in the body of Christ, and in the family of Christ. A pot stirrer will violate numbers 2 and 6 many times to achieve this.

It's pretty easy to see why the Lord detests these things, as do most righteous people. If you display any of these traits, now would be a good time to do some soul searching and to change your ways. Reading Proverbs is a good start.

WARNING AGAINST ADULTERY

20 My son, keep your father's command
     and do not forsake your mother's teaching.
21 Bind them always on your heart;
     fasten them around your neck.
22 When you walk, they will guide you;
     when you sleep, they will watch over you;
     when you awake, they will speak to you.
23 For this command is a lamp,
     this teaching is a light,
     and correction and instruction
     are the way of life,
24 keeping you from your neighbor's wife,
     from the smooth talk of the wayward woman.

So far, adultery has been covered in Proverbs 2, 5, and now here. So why does it keep coming up? Because adultery is one of the easiest, most desirous, and most wicked sins there is. As referenced in Proverbs 5, the path of the adulterous woman led the naive man straight to the grave. It causes the adulterer to lose his or her honor and dignity, and strangers will feast on his or her wealth after the divorce settlement.

For thousands of years, since the beginning of time, adultery has been destroying so many people, so many marriages, so many families, so much honor, and so much wealth that it is immeasurable. Take heed to the wisdom that is being offered. Don't mess with adultery, period.

> 25 Do not lust in your heart after her beauty
>   or let her captivate you with her eyes.

Don't lust after anyone if you're married. Lust is the beginning of the sin. Instead of being lured in, turn away, walk away, and remind yourself how much you love your spouse and your kids. Remind yourself that if you commit adultery with whoever you're lusting after, you will destroy your family, your spouse and your children. Remind yourself that it will lead to the loss of your honor, your wealth, and your life.

> 26 For a prostitute can be had for a loaf of bread,
>   but another man's wife preys on your very life.
> 27 Can a man scoop fire into his lap
>   without his cloths being burned?
> 28 Can a man walk on hot coals
>   without his feet being scorched?
> 29 So is he who sleeps with another man's wife,
>   no one who touches her will go unpunished.

This proverb is about sleeping with a married woman, another man's wife. If you have such a burning desire

Proverbs 6 59

to have sexual intercourse with a woman, "…a prostitute can be had for a loaf of bread…." In other words, leave the married woman alone and find an unmarried woman to have sex with. Proverbs is not promoting prostitution, but highlighting the point that there are other options that won't cost you your life.

Can a man scoop fire in his lap without his clothes being burned? Committing adultery with another man's wife is being compared to putting fire in your lap. How does a man not get burned by scooping fire into his lap? How does he not get burned by sleeping with another man's wife?

Sleeping with another man's wife is also compared to walking across hot coals. How can a man do that and not get his feet scorched? How does he not get scorched by sleeping with another man's wife? No one who touches her will go unpunished.

As previously discussed, sleeping with another man's wife is a death sentence from the woman's husband. Murder may be against today's law, but countless men have been killed by jealous husbands for sleeping with their wives.

> 30 People do not despise a thief if he steals
>   to satisfy his hunger when he is starving.
> 31 Yet if he is caught, he must pay sevenfold,
>   though it costs him all the wealth of his house.
> 32 But a man who commits adultery has no sense,
>   whoever does so destroys himself.

33 Blows and disgrace are his lot,
   and his shame will never be wiped away.
34 For jealousy arouses a husband's fury,
   and he will show no mercy when he takes revenge.
35 He will not accept any compensation;
   he will refuse any bribe, however great it is.

To a man, there is nothing worse than someone else sleeping with his wife. It is the most sacred thing to him. It is such a violation that his fury will be aroused, and he will show no mercy when he takes revenge. He wants nothing but to kill the adulterous man. He won't take a bribe; he won't take compensation; the man must die. That is the only compensation, and he is right. If his wife was a willing participant, many times she will be killed too for what is even a worse violation.

So, why put yourself in a situation where someone will relentlessly try to kill you, and that person is in the right for doing so? The temptation is great, the satisfaction is hollow, and the consequences are deadly. And if by some miracle you aren't killed by the jealous husband, everyone will find out, and you'll live a life of disgrace and dishonor. Why would any man want to associate with you? If you'll sleep with another man's wife, what's to stop you from trying to sleep with mine? As an adulterer, you are automatically a sleazy, dishonorable person; therefore, honorable people will not want to be associated with you.

PROVERBS 7

WARNING AGAINST THE ADULTEROUS WOMAN

1. My son, keep my words
   and store up my commands within you.
2. Keep my commands and you will live;
   guard my teachings as the apple of your eye.
3. Bind them on your fingers;
   write them on the tablet of your heart.
4. Say to wisdom, "You are my sister,"
   and to insight, "You are my relative."
5. They will keep you from the adulterous woman,
   from the wayward woman with her seductive words.

Once again, adultery rears its ugly head in Proverbs 7. All the repetition of this topic highlights how powerful and how dangerous adultery and the adulterous woman can be. To reiterate once again, sleeping with another man's wife equals death.

The word *wayward* in verse 5 means difficult to control or predict because of unusual or perverse behavior. At all costs, stay away from the adulterous and wayward woman and her seductive words.

> 6 At the window of my house
>   I looked down through the lattice.
> 7 I saw among the simple
>   I noticed among the young men,
>   a youth who had no sense.
> 8 He was going down the street near her corner
>   walking along in the direction of her house
> 9 at twilight, as the day was fading,
>   as the dark of night set in.

This proverb is about a naïve young man, "a youth who had no sense." He's walking down the street in the direction of the adulterous woman's house as dark is setting in. While it's possible he doesn't know she lives there and he really just happens to walk by, I don't think we can automatically assume that's the case. He may very well know a wayward woman lives there. He may know when she comes out to play. In any case, he just wants to partake in what he perceives as harmless sex.

> 10 Then out came a woman to meet him,
>   dressed like a prostitute and with crafty intent.
> 11 (She is unruly and defiant,
>   her feet never stay at home;

12 now in the street, now in the squares,
   at every corner she lurks.)
13 She took hold of him and kissed him
   and with a brazen face she said:

The wayward woman comes out to meet him, dressed very provocatively. She takes hold of the naïve boy, kisses him, and starts to seduce him with her provocative words.

14 "Today I fulfilled my vows,
   and I have food from my fellowship offering at home.
15 So I came out to meet you;
   I looked for you and have found you!
16 I have covered my bed
   With colored linens from Egypt.
17 I have perfumed by bed
   with myrrh, aloes and cinnamon.
18 Come, let's drink deeply of love till morning;
   let's enjoy ourselves with love!
19 My husband is not at home;
   he is gone on a long journey.
20 He took his purse filled with money
   and will not be home till full moon."

The adulterous woman has prepared her web to attract the naïve prey. Brazenly, this unruly and defiant woman admits she is married and that her husband is not home.

> 21 With persuasive words she led him astray;
>   she seduced him with her smooth talk.
> 22 All at once he followed her
>   like an ox going to the slaughter,
>   like a deer stepping into a noose
> 23 till an arrow pierces his liver,
>   like a bird darting into a snare,
>   little knowing it will cost him his life.

Being a naïve youth, he falls for her seductive words, not realizing the consequences. If this is you, you now have wisdom, knowledge, and some level of experience because you have heard the words of this proverb. Do not fall for her seductive words or ways. Do not even wait until she finishes the first sentence. Remove yourself from the situation immediately. You are walking into a trap that will cost you your life, "like an ox going to the slaughter."

> 24 Now then, my sons, listen to me;
>   pay attention to what I say.
> 25 Do not let your heart turn to her ways
>   or stray into her paths.
> 26 Many are the victims she has brought down;
>   her slain are a mighty throng.
> 27 Her house is a highway to the grave,
>   leading down to the chambers of death.

Again, listen to what I tell you; pay attention to what I say. Stay away from the wayward adulterous woman; don't stray into her path. Her victims are many and mighty. Walking on the path to her house, associating with her, and succumbing to her seductive ways is a highway to the grave. Just don't do it.

Proverbs 8

Wisdom's Call

1 Does not wisdom call out?
  Does not understanding raise her voice?
2 At the highest point along the way,
  where the paths meet, she takes her stand;
3 beside the gate leading into the city,
  at the entrance, she cries aloud:
4 "To you, O people, I call out;
  I raise my voice to all mankind.
5 You who are simple, gain prudence;
  you who are foolish, set your hearts on it.
6 Listen, for I have trustworthy things to say;
  I open my lips to speak what is right.
7 My mouth speaks what is true,
  for my lips detest wickedness.
8 All the words of my mouth are just;
  none of them is crooked or perverse.

9 To the discerning all of them are right;
    they are upright to those who have found knowledge.
10 Choose my instruction instead of silver,
    knowledge rather than choice gold,
11 for wisdom is more precious than rubies,
    and nothing you desire can compare with her.

Wisdom's call is contrasted against Proverbs 7's warning against the adulterous woman. Lady Wisdom guides us, helps us make wise choices, and succeed. Wisdom calls out and understanding raises her voice; we just need to be open to what she has to say.

In Solomon's time, the wise people of a community met at the gate to the city to dispense their wisdom, judge cases, and make policy. This was a place where people could go to hear and absorb wisdom, where they could ask questions and learn.

We can seek and absorb wisdom today, first by reading the book of Proverbs, and then by finding others who are wise and understanding. Once we meet these people, we can introduce ourselves and let them know our intentions are to gain wisdom and understanding. If they are truly wise and understanding, they will take the time to share it with us.

We need to set our hearts on wisdom and not to rest until we have received it. Wisdom and understanding have trustworthy things to say; they speak what is right, not what is wrong.

With wisdom, knowledge, and understanding we become smart enough to acquire silver; gold; and rubies, in abundance, the right way. Without wisdom, knowledge, and understanding we are far more likely to acquire these riches the wrong way.

Nothing we desire can compare with wisdom, knowledge, and understanding. With them, we can achieve more than we desire.

God's wisdom is trying to drive home a couple of points:

- Wisdom, knowledge, and understanding are incredibly important. We need to seek them out, gain them, live our lives by them, and never let them go.

- When we stay far away from those who entice us to adultery (i.e., the adulterous wayward woman), we demonstrate that we have wisdom, knowledge, and understanding. Adultery is a path to death.

12 I, wisdom, dwell together with prudence;
   I possess knowledge and discretion.
13 To fear the Lord is to hate evil;
   I hate pride and arrogance,
   evil behavior and perverse speech.
14 Counsel and sound judgement are mine;
   I have insight, I have power.
15 By me kings reign
   and rulers issue decrees that are just;
16 by me princes govern,
   and nobles – all who rule on earth.

17 I love those who love me,
   and those who seek me find me.
18 With me are riches and honor,
   enduring wealth and prosperity.
19 My fruit is better than fine gold;
   what I yield surpasses choice silver.
20 I walk in the way of righteousness,
   along the paths of justice,
21 bestowing a rich inheritance on those who love me
   and making their treasuries full.

Being *prudent* means acting with or showing care and thought for the future. It is similar to being wise or judicious. *Prudence* is simply the act of being prudent or wise.

Wisdom and prudence "dwell together." These are similar traits, accompanied by knowledge and discretion. The fear of the Lord is the beginning of knowledge and the foundation of wisdom. To fear the Lord is to hate evil, pride, arrogance, evil behavior, and perverse speech.

Wisdom brings with it counsel, sound judgment, insight, and power. These are used by kings and judges who issue decrees or judgments that are just, fair, and right. If we seek wisdom, we will find it. If we love wisdom, it will bring us riches, honor, enduring wealth, and prosperity. Instead of seeking the riches and honor, however, it's much better to seek the wisdom, because it is wisdom that bestows the rich inheritance on all who love it.

Proverbs 8

22 "The Lord brought me forth as the first of his works,
   before his deeds of old'
23 I was formed long ages ago,
   at the very beginning, when the world came to be.
24 When there were no watery depths, I was given birth,
   when there were no springs overflowing with water,
25 before the mountains were settled in place,
   before the hills, I was given birth,
26 before he made the world or its fields
   or any of the dust of the earth.
27 I was there when he set the heavens in place,
   when he marked out the horizon on the face of the deep,
28 when he established the clouds above
   and fixed securely the fountains of the deep,
29 when he gave the sea its boundary
   so the waters would not overstep his command,
   and when he marked out the foundations of the earth.
30 Then I was constantly at his side.
   I was filled with delight day after day,
   Rejoicing always in his presence,
31 rejoicing in his whole world
   and delighting in mankind.

Lady Wisdom was derived from God and has been with Him since He created the cosmos. Wisdom is both a characteristic and a gift from God, which we should seek. Once we find it, we should never let it go.

> 32 "Now then, my children, listen to me;
>   blessed are those who keep my ways.
> 33 Listen to my instruction and be wise;
>   do not disregard it.
> 34 Blessed are those who listen to me,
>   watching daily at my doors,
>   waiting at my doorway.
> 35 For those who find me find life
>   and receive favor from the Lord.
> 36 But those who fail to find me harm themselves;
>   all who hate me love death."

In this part of the proverb, Lady Wisdom shifts her focus from the simpletons to the generations of children who are willing to listen. Finding wisdom is a life-and-death decision. Those who listen, seek, and keep her ways are blessed and receive favor from the Lord. Those who do not will love death.

Proverbs 9

INVITATIONS OF WISDOM AND FOLLY

1 Wisdom has built her house;
  she has set up its seven pillars.
2 She has prepared her meat and mixed her wine;
  she has also set her table.
3 She has sent out her servants, and she calls
  from the highest point in the city,
4 "Let all who are simple come to my house!"
  To those who have no sense she says.
5 "Come, eat my food
  and drink the wine I have mixed.
6 Leave your simple ways and you will live;
  walk in the way of insight."

Lady Wisdom has built her house and is inviting all the simple, or the unwise, to come in and receive her feast of wisdom because anyone who dines on it will live. The seven pillars are figurative; they do not represent seven principles of wisdom. In the Bible, the number seven represents completeness and perfection. This verse poetically states that wisdom lacks nothing; it is complete and perfect.

> 7 Whoever corrects a mocker invites insults;
>   whoever rebukes the wicked incurs abuse.
> 8 Do not rebuke mockers or they will hate you;
>   rebuke the wise and they will love you.
> 9 Instruct the wise and they will be wiser still;
>   teach the righteous and they will add to their learning.

Mockers and wicked people don't like to be corrected because they think they already know it all. In fact, they will lash out, mock, and abuse us if we try to correct them. Those who are wise understand, however, that while they have a lot of knowledge, they do not know everything. In fact, those who are wise are always learning. They believe everyone on the planet can teach them something.

So, if a wise person says something that is wrong and someone corrects him or her, the wise person not only appreciates it, but contemplates it and seeks to change his or her views if they are incorrect. The wise person will also ask the one who corrected him or her what the correct view is. Those who are wise see the correction as an opportunity to learn something new.

> 10 The fear of the Lord is the beginning of wisdom,
>   and knowledge of the Holy One is understanding.
> 11 For through wisdom your days will be many,
>   and years will be added to your life.
> 12 If you are wise, your wisdom will reward you;
>   if you are a mocker, you alone will suffer.

Fear of the Lord is the beginning of wisdom. Knowledge of the Holy One is understanding. Wisdom will reward you with a long and prosperous life. It's important to note, however, that we cannot have wisdom and understanding without knowing and fearing the Lord. Mockers and fools, neither of whom know or fear the Lord, will lack wisdom and understanding and will suffer as a result.

> 13 Folly is an unruly woman;
>   she is simple and knows nothing.
> 14 She sits at the door of her house,
>   on a seat at the highest point of the city,
> 15 calling out to those who pass by,
>   who go straight on their way,
> 16 "Let all who are simple come to my house!"
>   To those who have no sense she says,
> 17 "Stolen water is sweet;
>   food eaten in secret is delicious!"
> 18 But little do they know that the dead are there,
>   that her guests are deep in the realm of the dead.

We have been talking about Lady Wisdom, and now here is Lady Folly sitting at the door of her house, calling out to those who pass by, much like the adulterous woman, the prostitute, luring in unsuspecting men and leading them to their deaths. Lady Folly is simple and will only try to seduce a man with sin. She offers her stolen food to eat in secret, which seems even more delicious than the banquet that Lady Wisdom is serving. Lady Folly's lifestyle titillates and demands no moral rectitude.

Sin is a funny thing. For the unwise, one sin often leads to other sins because the unwise find it satisfying to sin. The simple do not set out to do evil, but they stray into her house with no knowledge of what is right and wrong. The wise, on the other hand, keep their eyes fixed on the right path. They seek wisdom and recognize folly for what it is and avoid it at all costs.

Proverbs 10

Proverbs of Solomon

1 The proverbs of Solomon:
A wise son brings joy to his father,
but a foolish son brings grief to his mother.

A parent's primary job is to educate and raise his or her children properly. Having a wise son or daughter brings joy to the parents as they know they completed a job well done. Having a son or daughter who is foolish will prove to be a problem to the parents and bring them grief for the rest of their lives. Parents need to make the sacrifices necessary to spend time educating their children and raising them in a righteous and God-fearing way. There is an old saying that sticks with me: How do you spell love when it comes to your children? Time. Spend time with your children; you're going to blink and they will be gone.

> 2 Ill-gotten treasures have no lasting value,
> but righteousness delivers from death.

Stolen goods have no lasting value and will be lost. Righteousness and wisdom will keep us from crooked paths that lead to death and ruin.

> 3 The LORD does not let the righteous go hungry,
> but he thwarts the craving of the wicked.

Righteous people have a fear of the Lord and follow God. This gives them the power of the Holy Spirit to live righteous lives, which lends to a secure lifestyle.

> 4 Lazy hands make for poverty,
> but diligent hands bring wealth.

Sluggards, people who are lazy, will always be poor because they don't work. Those who are hard-working and diligent, on the other hand, will become wealthy because of their work ethic and skill.

> 5 He who gathers crops in summer is a prudent son,
> but he who sleeps during harvest is a disgraceful son.

During the time Proverbs was written, wealth meant a good harvest. So, at harvest time, it was "all hands on deck" to harvest the crop, which would take care of the family the entire next year. A son who helped bring in the harvest was a prudent son because he pulled his own weight. But a son who didn't work to help bring in the harvest was not contributing to the family's means of survival and well-being. Instead, he was relying on other family members to do it. Because he did not carry his own weight, he was a disgraceful son.

> 6 Blessings crown the head of the righteous,
>   but violence overwhelms the mouth of the wicked.

The righteous and the wise are blessed with wealth and prudence because they are smart and live a good life. Good things tend to happen to people who live that way. The wicked and the unwise, however, run their mouths and get themselves into violent trouble.

> 7 The name of the righteous is used in blessings,
>   but the name of the wicked will rot.

The names of the righteous will be remembered and revered, while the names of the wicked and the unwise will be forgotten.

> 8 The wise in heart accept commands,
>   but a chattering fool comes to ruin.

A wise person accepts direction, but fools do not accept commands. Instead they run their mouths and ultimately come to ruin.

9 Whoever walks in integrity walks securely,
   but whoever takes crooked paths will be found out.

A wise person, who lives a righteous lifestyle, stays on the straight path and walks securely. An unwise person, on the other hand, takes crooked paths, which ultimately lead to death and ruin. People who walk crooked paths are ultimately exposed.

10 Whoever winks maliciously causes grief,
   and a chattering fool comes to ruin.

Whether winking is a sexual come-on or a sign of getting over on someone, it produces feelings of discomfort in the other person. It also shows oneself as an arrogant fool having no judgment.

11 The mouth of the righteous is a fountain of life,
   but the mouth of the wicked conceals violence.

The words that come from a righteous person's mouth seek to help and promote life because they speak of good, Godly principles. The mouth of the wicked, on the other hand, conceals and spews words of violence.

12 Hatred stirs up conflict,
   but love covers over all wrongs.

Proverbs 10

Hatred is an attitude that circumvents innocent intentions. Love is an attitude that cherishes the wrongdoer as a friend to be won over, not as an enemy to get even with.

13 Wisdom is found on the lips of the discerning,
  but a rod is for the back of one who has no sense.

Discerning means showing insight and judgment (being perceptive). A discerning person is a wise person, which means he or she has knowledge and understanding. This is demonstrated by the words of wisdom he or she speaks.

The fool, who has no sense, runs about, chattering folly and violent words, and needs discipline, which in the time of Proverbs meant a beating with a rod.

14 The wise store up knowledge,
  but the mouth of a fool invites ruin.

The wise spend their entire lives seeking wisdom and knowledge. They know that learning does not stop after high school or college.

Fools are too lazy to seek knowledge, believing it is a waste of time. Instead they run their mouths and invite ruin.

15 The wealth of the rich is their fortified city,
  but poverty is the ruin of the poor.

Crops created wealth for the rich and gave them a form of security. The rich can find themselves poor, however, if they give in to folly and wickedness. Poverty can be difficult to get out of, but allowing the Lord to be our source of trust and confidence is a good start.

16 The wages of the righteous is life,
   but the earnings of the wicked are sin and death.

Wise and righteous people earn the wage of a good life and an everlasting life thereafter. The wages of the wicked, however, are sin, a poor life, and death.

17 Whoever heeds discipline shows the way to life,
   but whoever ignores correction leads others astray.

Whoever accepts correction shows the way to life. The wise accept correction and instruction and become wiser. But the person who ignores correction or discipline because they think they know better, ignores wisdom. As a result, this person will be led down a crooked path and will take others with him or her.

18 Whoever conceals hatred with lying lips
   and spreads slander is a fool.

A person who spreads lies about others is a wicked fool. This person has no wisdom and no fear of the Lord. He or she is destined down a crooked path that leads to death and ruin.

19 Sin is not ended by multiplying words,
   but the prudent hold their tongues.

Sinful and imprudent people run their mouths, trying to cover up a sinful situation. Prudent and wise people, however, keep their mouths shut and don't say anything to enflame a bad situation.

20 The tongue of the righteous is choice silver,
   but the heart of the wicked is of little value.

The righteous and wise speak words of truth and wisdom. They tell us the honest truth and not what they think we want to hear. The wicked person's heart and character have little value because they are corrupt.

21 The lips of the righteous nourish many,
   but fools die for lack of sense.

The words spoken by those who are righteous and wise spread wisdom to the simple, which helps make them wise, as well. In this way, they are able to achieve understanding and abundance. Fools die because, well, they're fools, and they'll walk down a crooked path leading to death and ruin.

22 The blessing of the LORD brings wealth,
   without painful toil for it.

God gives us as believers the ability to provide for ourselves and others. Those who are wise will use the abundance that God has given them and their families for themselves and others. Wealth doesn't become true wealth until it is used to help others overcome poverty and hunger.

> 23 A fool finds pleasure in wicked schemes,
>   but a person of understanding delights in wisdom.

Fools are dumb, and dumb people are always looking for get-rich-quick schemes. These are con jobs to take someone's money unjustly. It is yet another crooked path that leads to death and ruin. A person of understanding, however, delights in wisdom. As a result, he or she is always gaining more wisdom and dispensing it to others.

> 24 What the wicked dread will overtake them;
>   what the righteous desire will be granted.

Even though the wicked are petrified of death, they continually walk the crooked paths that lead them to the grave. Those who fear the Lord, however, are seeking salvation and eternal life with Him. This verse offers you a choice: having your own desires and fears come true, which will happen to those who reject God and live their own way, or accepting God's salvation and living His way, which leads to eternal life with Him.

Proverbs 10

> 25 When the storm has swept by, the wicked are gone,
> but the righteous stand firm forever.

Again, the wicked are fools and fools are not smart. They don't prepare for either an actual storm or a storm in life. As a result, the storms take them out. The righteous and wise, on the other hand, are prepared for what life throws at them, which means they will stand firm.

> 26 As vinegar to the teeth and smoke to the eyes,
> so are sluggards to those who send them.

Vinegar to the teeth and smoke to the eyes are irritating. If you send a sluggard (a lazy person) to do a job for you, you'll end up irritated because the job won't be done correctly, timely, or at all.

> 27 The fear of the LORD adds length to life,
> but the years of the wicked are cut short.

The fear of the Lord is the beginning of wisdom. Wisdom will keep us on the straight path of life. As we have seen, the wicked are fools and travel the crooked paths that lead to death and ruin.

> 28 The prospect of the righteous is joy,
> but the hopes of the wicked come to nothing.

The righteous have good things to look forward to because they have wisdom and understanding. They have wealth and prosperity because they walk the straight path and follow the Lord. Again, the wicked are dumb and they do dumb things. As a result, their hopes and dreams come up empty.

> 29 The way of the LORD is a refuge for the blameless,
> but it is the ruin of those who do evil.

The blameless are those who fear and trust in the Lord and find refuge in Him. They find that trusting in God and following His laws keeps them on the straight path of life. But those who do evil will follow crooked paths that lead to death and ruin.

> 30 The righteous will never be uprooted,
> but the wicked will not remain in the land.

The righteous and the wise, who fear the Lord, shall never be removed from their land. The wicked, on the other hand, will not remain in their land or inhabit the earth. Rather, they will be uprooted and removed.

> 31 From the mouth of the righteous comes the fruit of wisdom,
> but a perverse tongue will be silenced.

Those who are righteous and wise speak truth and wisdom; they do and say the right things. In speaking wisdom, they also spread wisdom to others who seek it. The wicked fool, the mocker who speaks perverse words, will meet his or her fate on a crooked path.

32 The lips of the righteous know what finds favor,
    but the mouth of the wicked only what is perverse.

As we have just seen, the wise and the righteous speak wisdom, and wisdom finds favor with them because it is right and just. The words that come from the wicked and the foolish, however, are perverse and will take them down a crooked path.

Proverbs 11

1 The LORD detests dishonest scales,
   but accurate weights find favor with him.

The Lord is the one who upholds moral order. Dishonest scales refer to a dishonest merchant who measures a lesser amount of the item than a customer is buying. The merchant may have a counterweight labeled 1lb, for example, that only weighs 0.9lbs. So, when he measures out 1lb of flour, the customer is really getting only 0.9lbs of flour, which is 10 percent less than the customer purchased. This makes the merchant a thief because he has stolen money from his customer, the very person who is keeping him in business. This merchant will not find favor with the Lord, but an honest merchant, who weighs his goods accurately and does not cheat his customers, will.

2 When pride comes, then comes disgrace,
   but with humility comes wisdom.

Pride means thinking we are better than everyone else when we are not. Pride gives us a false sense of who we are because we think we can do everything on our own and we don't need God or anyone else. Consequently, we go out on the preverbal limb, do something stupid, and end up falling on our faces. God hates pride. Refer back to Proverbs 8:13, which says, "To fear the Lord is to hate evil; I hate pride and arrogance, evil behavior and perverse speech."

Wisdom comes with humility, not pride. It's difficult, if not impossible, for a prideful person to become wise, because they think they already know it all. Consequently, they don't take the time to learn. They are too busy running their mouths, posting on social media, counting their likes, etc. to take a step back, examine themselves, and seek humility. The best thing we can do is close our mouths, open our ears and our eyes, and seek wisdom.

Review Proverbs 2:1-11 again.

3 The integrity of the upright guides them,
  but the unfaithful are destroyed by their duplicity.

Honor, integrity, and moral standards guide the righteous and the upright so that they stay on the straight paths.

The word *duplicity* means being deliberately deceptive or double dealing. The unfaithful, people who have no honor or moral standards and who do not fear the Lord, will be destroyed by their own deliberate deceptiveness.

> 4 Wealth is worthless in the day of wrath,
> but righteousness delivers from death.

The day of wrath is judgment day. That is the day God brings us before Him and judges us for all our deeds, good and bad. Most assume this is the day we pass from this earth. Some wealthy live by the code that the person who has the most money wins. But our wealth is not our own; it is God's. He has placed it with us while we are on this earth, hoping we will be good stewards of it.

So what have you done with the wealth and the wisdom that God has given you? Have you been a good steward of it? Have you helped those less monetarily fortunate than yourself? Have you used your wealth for good? Or have you stored it away and hoarded it?

We cannot take it with us when we pass from this earth, so wouldn't it be wise for us to use our wealth to do good and help others while we are here? Righteousness, fear of the Lord, wisdom, and understanding delivers us from death and offers us eternal life with God. So, on our day of judgment, we need to consider how we would like to be judged.

> 5 The righteousness of the blameless makes their paths straight,
> but the wicked are brought down by their own wickedness.

Once again, we have a reference to paths, straight ones followed by the righteous. The second half of the sentence infers that the wicked are not taking the straight path, but the crooked path. The blameless and righteous person, one who has wisdom, stays on the straight paths and out of trouble. Crooked paths, as we know, lead to death and ruin. This is the path the wicked walk down. As a result, the wicked person is brought down by his or her own schemes, duplicity, and wickedness.

> 6 The righteousness of the upright delivers them,
>   but the unfaithful are trapped by evil desires.

This verse is similar to 11:3. Discovering the fear of the Lord, following Him, reading the Bible, following God's law, and finding wisdom will give us understanding so we can become "un-trapped" by evil desires.

> 7 Hopes placed in mortals die with them;
>   all the promise of their power comes to nothing.

This refers to fearing the Lord and trusting in Him for our hopes and dreams. Hopes and dreams entrusted to mere mortals will die when we die.

> 8 The righteous person is rescued from trouble,
>   and it falls on the wicked instead.

God's people are not excluded from problems or struggles; in fact, we have them often. But the righteous person, one of wisdom and understanding, who walks the straight paths, is rescued from trouble, which tends to follow the wicked person, who walks the crooked paths.

> 9 With their mouths the godless destroy their neighbors,
> but through knowledge the righteous escape.

Words can build relationships or tear them down. Unfortunately, most of the time, the instincts of the unrighteous are to destroy rather than build. The unrighteous mindset says, "I must make that person look bad that he doesn't look better than me," or "I'm too lazy to improve myself, so I'll tear down my neighbor to make myself look better." The righteous can escape this, however, by staying on the straight path, and divorcing themselves from that wicked person.

> 10 When the righteous prosper, the city rejoices;
> when the wicked perish, there are shouts of joy.

When the righteous do well, they do things that benefit the city they live in, which helps all its citizens prosper and rejoice. When the wicked perish, they take their corruption with them, and the city and its people are better off.

> 11 Through the blessing of the upright a city is exalted,
> but by the mouth of the wicked it is destroyed.

Like verse 10, when the righteous do well they will do things to benefit their city and its citizens. But because the wicked can't stand to see the righteous do well, they will spread negative talk and lies to destroy the city.

> 12 Whoever derides their neighbor has no sense,
> but the one who has understanding holds their tongue.

To *deride* means to speak poorly of or to laugh at someone. This is what fools, senseless people, do. People with wisdom and understanding, on the other hand, hold their tongue and say nothing. Think of a situation where something unfortunate happens to your neighbor in front of the rest of the neighbors. The senseless person will laugh out loud and yell to your neighbor, in front of everyone, "You're stupid, and you deserve what happened to you!"

The wise person, the one who has understanding, will say nothing. This person will figure that your neighbor is already embarrassed in front of the entire community, so why belittle him or her and make the situation worse? Why tear an embarrassed person down further? The wise person says the right thing at the right time. Prudent silence matches prudent speech.

> 13 A gossip betrays a confidence,
> but a trustworthy person keeps a secret.

We all know the gossips in our community, the people who run around telling exaggerated stories and lies about others. They do this to look as though they are "in the know" and to stir up controversy. Some people just love drama because they think it's entertaining.

The gossip will take information in confidence, then turn to others and say, "I have something to tell you, but you have to promise not to tell anyone." They then tell the secret to others. But a trustworthy person, a wise person with understanding, keeps a secret.

When we accept information under the restriction of confidence, we are giving someone our word that we will not divulge the information. To break this promise is breaking our word and makes us untrustworthy and wicked.

14 For lack of guidance a nation falls,
    but victory is won through many advisers.

A wise leader knows what he or she knows, but more importantly, a wise leader knows what he or she doesn't know. No one can know everything and be an expert in every field. That's why a wise leader takes counsel from many smart advisors. The trick for the leader is to select advisors who are not biased and will not pursue an agenda.

Because the leaders can't know everything about a situation or a project, he or she may simply not have all the facts, or his or her initial instinct may be clouded in bias or misunderstanding. But after he or she considers all the facts from the wise advisors, he or she makes a decision.

15 Whoever puts up security for a stranger will surely suffer,
   but whoever refuses to shake hands in pledge is safe.

As we saw in Proverbs 6:1-5, this describes putting up security or something of value and shaking hands in pledge to pay another person's debt if that person doesn't pay. In today's world, this is co-signing a loan. Once the stranger has successfully shifted the burden of the debt off themselves and onto you, he or she will probably never repay it, and the entire responsibility for repayment will fall on you. Avoid the situation altogether and remain safe.

16 A kindhearted woman gains honor,
   but ruthless men gain only wealth.

The word *honor* means having a special esteem or respect, or having a good reputation. A gracious woman with inner beauty gains honor because she is polite, courteous, and wise. Ruthless people who go after money any way they can get it have no honor or wisdom. The wealth they gain will disappear quickly as a result of their way of life and poor decision making.

17 Those who are kind benefit themselves,
   but the cruel bring ruin on themselves.

The kind are on the path to wisdom, while the cruel are on a crooked path that leads to death and ruin.

> 18 A wicked person earns deceptive wages,
>   but the one who sows righteousness reaps a sure reward.

A wicked person earns "dirty money" often from doing illegal things. A person who has wisdom and lives a righteous life, on the other hand, reaps prosperity, honor, and righteousness.

> 19 Truly the righteous attain life,
>   but whoever pursues evil finds death.

As discussed many times, this refers to the wisdom of the paths. The righteous walk the straight path that leads to a life in harmony with the Lord and finds prosperity and understanding. The wicked, on the other hand, walk the crooked paths that lead to death and ruin.

> 20 The LORD detests those whose hearts are perverse,
>   but he delights in those whose ways are blameless.

A person who has a perverse heart has bottled up thoughts inside them that the Lord detests. But the Lord delights in those whose lives are free of perversion and evil.

> 21 Be sure of this: The wicked will not go unpunished,
>   but those who are righteous will go free.

The wicked will get punished, most of the time by walking down a crooked path and being done in by one of their own evil schemes. Those who live righteous lifestyles, however, stay on the straight paths and will live a long prosperous life as a result.

22 Like a gold ring in a pig's snout
   is a beautiful woman who shows no discretion.

This verse compares inner and outer beauty. People are often drawn to beautiful women or beautiful people in general simply because they are striking to look at. They are memorized by their beauty and see nothing else. Unfortunately, however, beautiful people are often arrogant and have a sense of entitlement. So their wickedness, indiscretion, lying, cheating, and vulgarity, quickly overtake their outer beauty.

When getting into a relationship, go with the person who is beautiful on the inside, someone who is kind and caring and full of wisdom, understanding, poise, and grace. Exterior beauty fades fast but inner beauty is forever.

Some folks have both inner and outer beauty, even though such a combination is rare. If you're fortunate to find yourself in a relationship with one, hold on to him or her with all you have. Regardless of how beautiful we are on the outside, we can all be, more importantly, beautiful on the inside.

23 The desire of the righteous ends only in good,
   but the hope of the wicked only in wrath.

The desires of the righteous will lead them down a straight path to things that are good, prosperous, and wise because their thoughts and their hearts are wise and desire wise things such as a spouse who is beautiful on the inside, wonderful children, a great career, a home, a secure retirement, and a happy life. The wicked, on the other hand, have hopes, thoughts, and dreams that lead them down crooked paths such as prostitution, underage sex, drugs, gambling, and get-rich-quick schemes.

24 One person gives freely, yet gains even more;
   another withholds unduly, but comes to poverty.
25 A generous person will prosper;
   whoever refreshes others will be refreshed.

Our possessions and our wealth are not really ours. God gave them to us and they belong to Him. We must be good stewards of the wealth He has given us until He returns to see what we have done with it. When we give freely of our wealth and possessions to help others, God will give us even greater wealth so that we can give more.

Giving frees us from our enslavement to our possessions and our money. A person who hordes his or her money and does not give some of it to the needy is a slave to the money and will ultimately lose it. The Bible suggests tithing, or giving, 10 percent of the "first fruits" the best of what we have of our income, to the needy, not what's left over at the end of the month or at the end of the year.

> 26 People curse the one who hoards grain,
>   but they pray God's blessing on the one who is willing to sell.

Grain from the harvest is a form of wealth. This verse depicts a person who has stored a lot of grain during a famine or a lean time. If the person sells some of that grain to the community, then the entire community will have food for themselves and their livestock. This is provided the person sells the grain at a fair price, demonstrating that he or she cares more about the community than his or her bank balance. God's people will pray blessings on a person who does this.

> 27 Whoever seeks good finds favor,
>   but evil comes to one who searches for it.

Trouble and evil are around every corner. A person who looks for trouble will have no problem finding the crooked path that leads to death and ruin. Instead, we must walk the straight path that leads to wisdom, prosperity, and favor. If we have evil in our hearts, it is never too late to change. We can still break the cycle and seek wisdom.

> 28 Those who trust in their riches will fall,
>   but the righteous will thrive like a green leaf.

Proverbs 3:5-6 says, "Trust in the Lord with all your heart and lean not on your own understanding; in all your ways submit to him, and he will make your paths straight." We spent a lot of time discussing this while studying Proverbs 3, so please go back and review it. People who trust in their riches worship their money and their wealth like an idol, instead of worshiping the Lord. Note the first two commandments:

1 You shall have no other gods before me.
2 You shall not make for yourself an image in the form of anything in heaven above or on the earth beneath or in the waters below. You shall not bow down to them or worship them; for I, the Lord your God, am a jealous God, punishing the children for the sin of the parents to the third and fourth generation of those who hate me, but showing love to a thousand generations of those who love me and keep my commands.

God spoke these words. He gave the 10 commandments for all the people to follow. These first two commandments clearly highlight that God wants to be number one in everyone's heart.

In Exodus 32, the people of Israel were waiting for Moses, who was with God on Mt. Sinai. While they were waiting, they got together, contributed their gold earrings, melted them down, and formed them into the likeness of a golden calf. Then they bowed down to it and worshiped it. This made God extremely angry.

Trusting in our riches and wealth before trusting in God is the same thing. We would be worshiping another god, our wealth and riches, before worshiping God, or Yahweh. The first part of the second commandment says that God is a jealous God, punishing people and their families for generations for the sin of hating Him, "…but the righteous will thrive like a green leaf," as the second part of Proverbs 11:28 says. The last portion of the second commandment says God will show "…love to a thousand generations of those who love me and keep my commands."

So, the bottom line is that righteous people who love God will thrive like a green leaf, prosper, become wise, and have understanding and wealth.

> 29 Whoever brings ruin on their family will inherit only wind,
> and the fool will be servant to the wise.

One of the greatest resources that God gives us is our families because they provide us with encouragement, support, acceptance, guidance, and counsel. We should all offer love and support to our families. To bring ruin, disgrace, or trouble into our families destroys one of the best assets we have and will only get us ostracized from them. As a result, we "…will inherit only the wind…" because someone else will get our inheritance.

Fools are servants to the wise because the wise are smart and fools are not. So, the not-so-smart people end up being servants to the smart people. So, why not become wise instead of a fool?

30 The fruit of the righteous is a tree of life,
   and the one who is wise saves lives.

The righteous display their wisdom and way of life, which others are attracted to. They see those who are wise and wonder how they can obtain wisdom for themselves and find meaning in their own lives. We can save the lives of others by bringing people to wisdom and understanding and keeping them off the crooked paths.

31 If the righteous receive their due on earth,
   how much more the ungodly and the sinner!

Even righteous people are sinners, and sinners get punished for their sins. The righteous and faithful know they will receive their remedial punishments while they are still on earth and that they will spend eternity in heaven with God. In contrast, the ungodly and unrighteous sinners will receive their harsh punishments on earth and remain on earth for eternity to experience them.

PROVERBS 12

1 Whoever loves discipline loves knowledge,
   but whoever hates correction is stupid.

If we have no willingness to learn, then attending school for many years will be a waste. But if we have a willingness to learn, there is no limit to what we can master. We must also be willing to accept correction and discipline to obtain wisdom from the wise.

2 Good people obtain favor from the LORD,
   but he condemns those who devise wicked schemes.

Devising wicked schemes was discussed during our study of Proverbs 1:11, so please refer back to that passage. Fools will go down a crooked path and say, "Come along with us; let's lie in wait for innocent blood, let's ambush some harmless soul; let's swallow them alive, like the grave...."

And what happens to them? Proverbs 1:18, "These men lie in wait for their own blood; they ambush only themselves! Such are the paths of all who go after ill-gotten gain; it takes away the life of those who get it." Righteous people seeking wisdom stay on the straight path and obtain favor from the Lord.

> 3 No one can be established through wickedness,
>   but the righteous cannot be uprooted.

To be established means to be successful the right way. It means playing by the rules and treating family and employees fairly. Some people choose to get ahead by cheating the system at every turn. Since they obtain their wealth by wicked means, they are not truly established. The righteous, the ones who achieve wealth and wisdom the right way are established, honored, and cannot be uprooted.

> 4 A wife of noble character is her husband's crown,
>   but a disgraceful wife is like decay in his bones.

The word *noble* means having or showing qualities of high moral character, such as courage, generosity, or honor. Any husband who has a wife who demonstrates these qualities would proudly display her like a king wears his crown.

The word *disgrace*, by contrast, means a loss of honor, respect, or reputation; shame. A husband who has a wife who demonstrates a disgraceful character is embarrassed and shamed. As a result, he would try to hide her.

> 5 The plans of the righteous are just,
>   but the advice of the wicked is deceitful.

The righteous and wise have goodness in their hearts. So, the things they plan are righteous and wise. The wicked, on the other hand, give deceitful and wicked advice to lure people down their crooked paths.

> 6 The words of the wicked lie in wait for blood,
>   but the speech of the upright rescues them.

The speech of the wicked attempts to lay a trap to kill the unsuspecting. The speech of the righteous and upright, on the other hand, redirects and saves others.

> 7 The wicked are overthrown and are no more,
>   but the house of the righteous stands firm.

The wicked end up dead, most likely because of their own schemes and folly. The righteous and wise, on the other hand, stay on the straight path and build their houses (i.e., their lives) on firm foundations so they will last.

8 A person is praised according to their prudence,
   and one with a warped mind is despised.

The word *prudence* means being cautious. A person who handles life cautiously is praised. Those who approach their lives with a reckless and evil attitude, however, have warped, evil, and vulgar desires. Such people and their desires are despised.

9 Better to be a nobody and yet have a servant
   than pretend to be somebody and have no food.

This verse refers to someone putting on a false appearance, most likely regarding how much wealth he or she has. Pretending to be better than you are costs money. You must drive an expensive car, live in an expensive house, and belong to the expensive clubs. Everyone thinks you're rich, but you have no money even for food and are in dept up to your eyeballs.

Be who you are, live within your means, and you will be able to hire servants to assist you with your life and your labor.

10 The righteous care for the needs of their animals,
    but the kindest acts of the wicked are cruel.

Back in the time of the book of Proverbs, using animals to work the land was a means of living and prospering. Caring for our animals is like putting oil in our tractors (that is, for those of us who have tractors today). When we take care of the tractor, it takes care of us. The acts of the wicked, however, are cruel and malicious and do not serve the greater good of their communities.

> 11 Those who work their land will have abundant food,
> but those who chase fantasies have no sense.

As referenced in verse 12:10, working the land to grow crops to sell, eat, or trade is how one lived and prospered. This is hard and steadfast work. But those who did the work, in most cases, had abundant food to eat and to sell. That gave families money to live on.

Chasing fantasies or get-rich-quick schemes, on the other hand, will get us nothing. They are most likely offered by wicked people looking to send us down crooked paths.

> 12 The wicked desire the stronghold of evildoers,
> but the root of the righteous endures.

A gang is a group of wicked people who create strongholds that thrive on fear, intimidation, mayhem, and killing. Gang members feed off the wickedness of the other members. They give each other support and inspire one another's evil deeds. As referenced many times, they will take their lives down crooked paths to death and ruin. Most gang members end up in one of two places: prison or the grave.

The righteous, on the other hand, place their roots in the Lord, goodness, and wisdom. They stay on the straight path and are around to play the long game.

> 13 Evildoers are trapped by their sinful talk,
> and so the innocent escape trouble.

People who lie most often get trapped in their own lies. They have to tell more lies to try to get out of the first lie, creating a tangled web of lies. Liars normally face some form of punishment, from losing a friend to jail time, when they are caught. The most obvious punishment is the dishonor they face because their communities perceived them as dishonest.

Let's let the truth set us free. If we simply refrain from lying, we'll never have to worry about getting caught and trying to cover up lies with more lies.

> 14 From the fruit of their lips people are filled with good things,
> and the work of their hands brings them reward.

Righteous people whose hearts are filled with goodness, love, and wisdom speak positive, healing, loving, and productive words. Their speech produces goodness in themselves, others, and their communities. The righteous and the wise also do good work, which brings them an honest reward.

> 15 The way of fools seems right to them,
> but the wise listen to advice.

As discussed earlier, fools are people who think they know it all and don't want any advice from anyone. The wise, on the other hand, understand that they don't know everything, but they are open to taking advice from smarter and more experienced people or seeking out information themselves so they can make the right decisions and so that can learn more and become wiser. In today's world of technology, the information is out there. We just have to seek the knowledge and wisdom.

> 16 Fools show their annoyance at once,
> but the prudent overlook an insult.

When annoyed or insulted, a fool is quick to fly off the handle and retaliate with another insult, which only enflames the situation. The wise and prudent, on the other hand, pause and think about how best to handle the situation. Maybe it is by having no response at all, or by uttering a quiet, yet confident, response that will achieve positive results. Proverbs 15:1 says, "A gentle answer turns away wrath."

> 17 An honest witness tells the truth,
> but a false witness tells lies.

The ninth commandment from God states, "You shall not give false testimony against your neighbor." Telling a lie about someone to the community or to an authority figure to get your neighbor in trouble or to tear them down is a sin and pure evil. An honest and wise person, on the other hand, always tells the truth. Remember, Proverbs 12:13 tells us to let the truth set us free.

> 18 The words of the reckless pierce like swords,
>   but the tongue of the wise brings healing.

There is an old saying: the pen is mightier than the sword. From the pen come words. Reckless and hurtful words have a way of piercing a person's heart, spirit, and soul. The wise, on the other hand, use positive, helpful, and healing words to pierce a person's soul in a positive and healing way.

The wise are always building people up. The evil are always tearing people down.

> 19 Truthful lips endure forever,
>   but a lying tongue lasts only a moment.

Truthful lips mean truthful words endure forever. These proverbs, written thousands of years ago, have endured the test of time. A lying tongue, on the other hand, means lying words never last because they are always found out. When a lie is discovered, it is discredited and dismissed.

> 20 Deceit is in the hearts of those who plot evil,
> but those who promote peace have joy.

The word *deceit* is the act of being deliberately misleading or deceptive. Sinful people have evil, deceitfulness, and malice in their hearts. Wise, righteous people, on the other hand, promote peace and have joy and happiness in their hearts. Given the choice, which would you prefer?

> 21 No harm overtakes the righteous,
> but the wicked have their fill of trouble.

The righteous and wise walk the straight path, which generally keeps them out of trouble, though sometimes even they experience harm. But when they do, they can use God's wisdom to see opportunities and move forward in a positive fashion. The wicked, by contrast, have none of God's wisdom and are therefore not equipped to handle their problems.

> 22 The LORD detests lying lips,
> but he delights in people who are trustworthy.

Liars are deceitful and evil people who are always starting trouble and plotting schemes. The Lord detests both the lies and the liars who spread them. But the Lord loves trustworthy, righteous people who tell the truth and spread goodness and light.

> 23 The prudent keep their knowledge to themselves,
> but a fool's heart blurts out folly.

The prudent and wise have a modest, self-confident demeanor. They have no need to show off or blurt out their knowledge to prove to everyone that they know what is going on. Fools, however, are insecure and have a constant need to prove themselves. Because they have no wisdom, they blurt out folly to let everyone believe they are smart and have the answer.

Unfortunately, all their efforts only show everyone they are fools because what they blurt out is most often wrong. While the prudent may not be noticed immediately, they will be respected later.

> 24 Diligent hands will rule,
> but laziness ends in forced labor.

The word *diligent* means having or showing care and conscientiousness in our work or duties. Those who have diligent hands will succeed and be promoted. They will be successful and self-sufficient. Those who do not work or do their work poorly, on the other hand, will fail and not be self-sufficient.

These people may take crooked paths to make that fast dollar and end up in prison. In ancient times, they would have ended up as someone's slave.

25 Anxiety weighs down the heart,
   but a kind word cheers it up.

The word *anxiety* is a feeling of worry, nervousness, or unease, typically about an imminent event or something that has an uncertain outcome. Anxiety wears on us; it brings us down with a feeling of dread. But a kind word helps relieve the anxiety.

26 The righteous choose their friends carefully,
   but the way of the wicked leads them astray.

Our friends have a big influence on how we think and act. A couple of old sayings come to mind: birds of a feather flock together, and lay down with dogs and you'll get fleas. People normally become like those they hang out with, which means our close friends influence our thinking and decision making. This is why righteous and wise people choose to hang out with other wise people so they can grow in their own wisdom. They choose to associate with people who act in a righteous manner so they can stay on the straight path.

The fool, on the other hand, associates with evil and wicked people, other fools, and ends up on the crooked path that leads to death and ruin.

27 The lazy do not roast any game,
   but the diligent feed on the riches of the hunt.

The lazy are too lazy to hunt for game to feed themselves and their families. If they do go hunting, they are too lazy to prepare for the hunt and conduct it in a skillful and diligent manner. This will result in little to no game being secured.

The diligent, on the other hand, hone their hunting skills so they can feed their families. As a result, they and their families feast on the riches of the hunt.

28 In the way of righteousness there is life;
    along that path is immortality.

The word *immorality* means having the ability to live forever, eternal life. In this instance we assume that eternal life is with God in heaven. The symbolism of "paths" is used throughout Proverbs. The straight path of the righteous, the wise, and the prosperous is contrasted with the crooked paths that lead to death and ruin for those who are wicked and evil.

Proverbs 13

1 A wise son heeds his father's instruction,
but a mocker does not respond to rebukes.

As we have observed, many of the proverbs start out with a father trying to instruct his son in wisdom. Let's recall the following:

- Proverbs 2:1-8: "My son, if you accept my words and store up my commands within you, turning your ear to wisdom and applying your heart to understanding – indeed, if you call out for insight and cry aloud for understanding, and if you look for it as for silver and search for it as for hidden treasure, you then will understand the fear of the Lord and find the knowledge of God. For the Lord gives wisdom; from his mouth come knowledge and understanding. He holds success in store for the upright, he is a shield to those whose walk is blameless, for he guards the course of the just and protects the way of his faithful ones."

- Proverbs 3:1-2: "My son, do not forget my teaching, but keep my commands in your heart, for they will prolong your life many years and bring you peace and prosperity."

- Proverbs 5:1-2: "My son, pay attention to my wisdom, turn your ear to my words of insight, that you may maintain discretion and your lips may preserve knowledge."

A *rebuke* is an expression of sharp disapproval or criticism because of someone's behavior or action. A wise son heeds his father's instruction and wisdom, but a mocker, a fool, does not listen or respond to his father's rebukes.

> 2 From the fruit of their lips people enjoy good things,
>   but the unfaithful have an appetite for violence.

Righteous words or speech can produce bounty and prosperity so we can have and enjoy good things. The wicked and unfaithful, on the other hand, live on crooked paths and therefore have a propensity toward violence, which will lead them to death and ruin.

> 3 Those who guard their lips preserve their lives,
>   but those who speak rashly will come to ruin.

A wise person has mastered the skill of self-control, not blurting out every thought as it jumps into his or her brain. It's best to be wise and stop and think before we speak or react. Blurting out a harsh comment or criticism about someone or their loved ones may cause the person to want to harm or kill you.

> 4 A sluggard's appetite is never filled,
> but the desires of the diligent are fully satisfied.

Lazy people crave everything but get little because they are lazy. Those who are diligent, however, go after their desires and work hard to achieve them so they can be fully satisfied.

> 5 The righteous hate what is false,
> but the wicked make themselves a stench
> and bring shame on themselves.

The righteous person hates lying, but a liar has no self-respect and does not take care of himself or herself. Because of this, he or she has bad breath and bad body odor. Such a person brings shame upon himself or herself and doesn't care.

> 6 Righteousness guards the person of integrity,
> but wickedness overthrows the sinner.

Righteousness and wisdom go hand in hand. That's why Proverbs instructs us to seek out and find wisdom and never let it go. It will protect us, keep us on the straight path, and help us make good choices. Every choice for good sets in motion another opportunity for good. The crooked path that leads to death and ruin, on the other hand, will overtake the wicked.

> 7 One person pretends to be rich, yet has nothing;
> another pretends to be poor, yet has great wealth.

This verse sounds like Proverbs 12:9, which we read earlier, so please refer back to that proverb and its commentary. A couple of sayings come to mind: fake it till you make it and keeping up with the Joneses. In an effort to climb the social ladder, a person may pretend to be rich to gain admiration and respect from other people and the community. But keeping up with the Joneses is a game no one can win because someone always has more money, a bigger house, or nicer cars than we have.

A humble person, by contrast, does not care about climbing the social ladder or impressing his or her friends. This person lives below his or her means in a modest home and drives a modest car. He or she does not belong to a club and has money left over at the end of each month, which the humble person invests. Such a person creates great wealth and lives a prosperous, yet modest, life.

By all means, we should try to improve ourselves by going to school and seeking and finding wisdom. But we also need to be happy with who we are.

8 A person's riches may ransom their life,
   but the poor cannot respond to threatening rebukes.

One of the risks people with wealth face when they show off how much money they have is being hunted down and killed by evil people, or even by someone they love, all for a ransom. The poor, however, have no wealth to meet such a demand.

9 The light of the righteous shines brightly,
   but the lamp of the wicked is snuffed out.

The reference to light in this verse means a person's spirit or heart. The light of the righteous shines brightly and is full of joy, while the light of the wicked and their entire lamp (their spirit and their heart) is snuffed out because they have lived a wicked dark life. The crooked paths they travel lead to death and ruin.

10 Where there is strife, there is pride,
   but wisdom is found in those who take advice.

There are many references in the Bible to God hating pride. The proud and the arrogant love themselves and their possessions more than God, that is, if they love God at all. Proverbs 8:13 says, "To fear the Lord is to hate evil; I hate pride and arrogance, evil behavior and perverse speech." People who are proud and arrogant will experience strife because they think they are too smart to seek advice and will go about things their own way. Even people who already have wisdom continue to seek it their entire lives. They take advice from other wise people, process it, and learn from it.

> 11 Dishonest money dwindles away,
> but whoever gathers money little by little makes it grow.

Dishonest money is money gained by illegal or unjust means. Its value is not recognized because the one who obtained it did not earn it honestly. As a result, that person will squander it on foolish things until it is gone.

The righteous and honest person, on the other hand, the one who earns money little by little, saves it, and invests it can make it grow. Compound interest can make the modest saver very wealthy over time. Please read the online white paper titled, "Rich Man, Poor Man" by Richard Russell. He does an amazing job of explaining the power of compound interest.

> 12 Hope deferred makes the heart sick,
> but a longing fulfilled is a tree of life.

A wish or an expectation that is delayed causes pain to the one who wished for it. A wish or an expectation that comes true, however, is a delight and a refreshment that makes the person's heart happy, extending his or her life.

13 Whoever scorns instruction will pay for it,
   but whoever respects a command is rewarded.

As referenced in Proverbs 1:7, fools reject instruction because they think they know it all. As a result, they will make foolish decisions and pay for them. The wise, however, is rewarded for taking instruction and respecting authority.

14 The teaching of the wise is a fountain of life,
   turning a person from the snares of death.

As referenced in Proverbs 1:5, "the wise listen and add to their learning." Learning is a lifelong endeavor. It doesn't stop after a person graduates from high school or college. In fact, for the wise, that is only the beginning of their learning. Those who turn from learning are fools who often walk crooked paths and make bad choices.

15 Good judgment wins favor,
   but the way of the unfaithful leads to their destruction.

Wise people have good judgment and therefore make good decisions and win favor with their families and communities. These people live right, are not arrogant, follow the ten commandments, have the fear of the Lord, and don't commit adultery. The ways of the unfaithful are those who have no fear of the Lord and no wisdom. These people are fools who walk the crooked paths that lead to death, ruin, and ultimately their own destruction.

> 16 All who are prudent act with knowledge,
>   but fools expose their folly.

The word *folly* means a lack of good sense or foolishness. People who have wisdom and knowledge act in a prudent and responsible manner. Fools, on the other hand, act in an irresponsible manner and show off their folly.

> 17 A wicked messenger falls into trouble,
>   but a trustworthy envoy brings healing.

The word *envoy* means a messenger or representative, especially one on a diplomatic mission. In the days of the proverbs, kings and other people had to rely on messengers to receive information. These messengers needed to be trustworthy and quick to deliver the correct information because inaccurate or delayed messages could have led to war and bloodshed. If the message received is altered in any way, it could have devastating effects on people's lives, their marriages, and their businesses.

    A trustworthy envoy brings healing by delivering the correct message in a timely fashion.

    Most people today get their news from online sources. This includes traditional news sources that are now online: Fox News, *The Washington Post*, *The New York Times*, Inside NOVA, etc.

Sadly most of our envoys today are wicked messengers who promote the search results and the news stories that meet their agenda. Most of the time this involves politics, which include attempts to sway an election from one candidate to another. Some of these wicked messengers will go out of business and some will have their monopolies broken up and become regulated.

It's important that we become wise and not consume all our information from one source. We need to listen to both sides of an issue and make up our own minds instead of listening to the sources who try to tell everyone what is true by spreading false information. Don't follow the herd. Make your own wise, rational, and well-informed decisions.

> 18 Whoever disregards discipline comes to poverty and shame,
> but whoever heeds correction is honored.

As we discussed earlier, a fool disregards instruction and discipline. Discipline is a method of trying to make someone learn the correct way. Fools disregard this because they think they already know everything. As a result, they end up in poverty and shame and on the crooked path that leads to death and ruin.

The person on the wise track, on the other hand, accepts correction, stays on the straight path, and is honored by his or her family and community.

19 A longing fulfilled is sweet to the soul,
    but fools detest turning from evil.

A longing fulfilled is a goal or a desire that is finally achieved. Once achieved it makes the person who achieved it happy and is sweet to the soul. These achievements might include an educational degree, a promotion, a new job, a new home, or a family.

Fools, on the other hand, long after unrighteous and evil goals. These are often schemes to get rich quick, which take them down the crooked path.

20 Walk with the wise and become wise,
    for a companion of fools suffers harm.

As referenced in Proverbs 12:26, friends have a big influence on how we act and think, so please go back and review that verse and the accompanying commentary.

21 Trouble pursues the sinner,
    but the righteous are rewarded with good things.

The sinners walk the crooked path. The crooked path leads to trouble and ultimately death and ruin.

God-fearing people, on the other hand, stay on the straight path and are rewarded with good things such as wisdom, a long and healthy life, a family, and prosperity.

22 A good person leaves an inheritance for their
    children's children,
  but a sinner's wealth is stored up for the righteous.

A righteous person leads a good life of working hard, gaining wisdom, saving and investing their money, and ultimately becoming wealthy. When they leave this earth for an eternal life with the Lord, they have an inheritance that they can give to their children and grandchildren, an inheritance that may continue to grow.

A sinner's wealth, on the other hand, is stored up for the righteous, which means they are going to mess up and lose the wealth they have accumulated, "…lest strangers feast on your wealth and your toil enrich the house of another," Proverbs 5:10. This proverb refers to a sinner who commits adultery and loses his or her wealth to strangers who will then feast on it and enrich their homes with it. Adultery, however, is only one way sinners mess up and lose their wealth.

The wise and prosperous investor, in contrast, always has liquid cash available to scoop up the deal at a fire sale price.

23 An unplowed field produces food for the poor,
    but injustice sweeps it away.

The poor are often victims of an unjust society. An unplowed field symbolizes a field the poor grow food on, with or without the owner's permission, because the owner didn't plant it. So, injustice, possibly the owner of the field, comes in and takes it away since it was grown on his or her property.

It's difficult for the poor to break out and get over that first hurdle of success that will allow them to achieve. They are always living hand to mouth. Righteous people need to do what they can to help the poor, and correct injustices, and the poor need to do what they can to help themselves. The single best way they can help themselves is to get an education. That is the key to breaking the cycle of poverty.

> 24 Whoever spares the rod hates their children,
>   but the one who loves their children is careful to discipline them.

The greatest responsibility that God gives parents is to teach and guide their children. A parent striking his or her child with a rod describes a parent disciplining the child to teach him or her to do good and to stay off the crooked path. Parents who don't take the time or effort to discipline their child "hate" the child because they are allowing that child to wander down the crooked path to death and ruin. Parents who discipline their children, on the other hand, love them because they are teaching them to stay on the straight path that leads to righteousness. Disciplining children when they are young will avert disaster in the future.

25 The righteous eat to their hearts' content,
   but the stomach of the wicked goes hungry.

The righteous live a good life, work hard, and save and invest their money. That is why they don't go hungry and live a prosperous life.

The wicked, however, live a wicked life of trouble and evil. They often never become prosperous, or they lose their prosperity and go hungry.

Proverbs 14

1 The wise woman builds her house,
   but with her own hands the foolish one tears hers down.

The wise woman embodies moral strength and righteousness. She works for the benefit of her family and her community. The foolish woman, on the other hand, is lazy and sinful and leads herself and others down the crooked path. In the process, she loses her family's home.

2 Whoever fears the LORD walks uprightly,
   but those who despise him are devious in their ways.

Wisdom is what the proverbs are all about, and if we seek it and find it, we will lead righteous lives. The fear of the Lord is the beginning of this process as we can recall from the proverbs we've already read:

- Proverbs 1:7: "The fear of the Lord is the beginning of knowledge, but fools despise wisdom and instruction."

- Proverbs 1:2-6: "(Purpose and Theme of the Proverbs)…for gaining wisdom and instruction; for understanding words of insight; for receiving instruction in prudent behavior, doing what is right and just and fair; for giving prudence to those who are simple, knowledge and discretion to the young – let the wise listen and add to their learning, and let the discerning get guidance – for understanding proverbs and parables, and the sayings and riddles of the wise."

- Proverbs 2:1-8: "My son, if you accept my words and store up my commands within you, turning your ear to wisdom and applying your heart to understanding – indeed, if you call out for insight and cry aloud for understanding, and if you look for it as for silver and search for it as for hidden treasure, then you will understand the fear of the Lord and find the knowledge of God. For the Lord gives wisdom, from his mouth come knowledge and understanding. He holds success in store for the upright, he is a shield to those whose walk is blameless, for he guards the course of the just and protects the way of his faithful ones."

Those who do not have the fear of the Lord are either ignorant of Him or despise Him. Those who despise the Lord are wicked people who walk the crooked paths and live devious lives.

> 3 A fool's mouth lashes out with pride,
> but the lips of the wise protect them.

Fools are arrogant and insecure. They profess to know it all and don't like to be challenged because they really don't know it all but want to keep the arrogant perception that they do. So, when someone challenges them, they lash out with a physical or verbal attack to take the focus off of their lack of knowledge and put that focus on something else. The wise, on the other hand, are humble and they choose their words wisely. This is what protects them.

> 4 Where there are no oxen, the manger is empty,
> but from the strength of an ox come abundant harvests.

In the time of Proverbs, oxen were used to plow the fields. This is how the farmers grew their crops and fed their families. It also created a form of currency as they would trade the crops for other goods and services. So, their crops were truly the lifeblood of their society.

If a farmer was without an ox, however, the manger (life) was empty because the farmer had nothing. From the strength of an ox came abundant harvests.

In our society today we don't use oxen to plow the fields since crops are mass produced using elaborate tractors and farming equipment. But in this riddle, the strength of an ox can be interpreted as the fear of the Lord. If we have no fear of the Lord, our manger is empty, which means our homes and our lives are empty. With the fear of the Lord, however, we will have an abundant harvest, которое means full homes and full lives filled with love, wisdom, and prosperity.

> 5 An honest witness does not deceive,
>   but a false witness pours out lies.

Again, the ninth commandment states, "You shall not give false testimony against your neighbor." Giving false testimony, which means lying about others, is wicked, evil, and against God's law. Giving false testimony can cause wrongful imprisonment or even death.

The honest and righteous person, however, tells the truth and does not try to deceive anyone.

> 6 The mocker seeks wisdom and finds none,
>   but knowledge comes easily to the discerning.

The word discerning means having or showing good judgment. Mockers seek wisdom but find none because they are not seeking it seriously enough. They have a foolish attitude and cannot seize wisdom.

Those who are discerning and have humble attitudes, on the other hand, easily find knowledge and wisdom because they pay attention and have attitudes that embrace learning. This is why we need to humble ourselves and embrace knowledge.

> 7 Stay away from a fool,
> for you will not find knowledge on their lips.

As referenced in Proverbs 12:26 and again in 13:20, our friends have a big influence on how we think and act. We normally assimilate, or become like, the people we hang out with. Our close friends will influence our thinking and decision making. This is the reason righteous and wise people choose to hang out with other wise people so they can gain in their own wisdom. They choose to associate with other righteous people so they can maintain the straight path.

The fool, on the other hand, becomes friends with evil and wicked people, other fools, and ends up on the crooked path to death and ruin.

> 8 The wisdom of the prudent is to give thought to their ways,
> but the folly of fools is deception.

A person who is wise and prudent consciously and deliberately acts righteously, honorably, and with compassion. What fools believe to be prudent is really folly and deception. They put no thought into their actions, which is why they are fools.

> 9 Fools mock at making amends for sin,
>   but goodwill is found among the upright.

The word *repentance* means the action of sincere regret or remorse. Fools enjoy making fun of what other people do. Everyone is a sinner, but the wise, the righteous, those who fear the Lord understand that and confess their sins to the Lord in prayer. They seek repentance and ask for forgiveness in the Lord's name, in the name of Jesus Christ.

Fools have no fear of the Lord, or any sense for that matter. In an arrogant fit of insecurity, the fool will mock the faithful, because they have none, in order to make themselves look better, without having to work for it.

Goodwill, however, is found among the upright. These are the righteous and wise people who live a good and positive life, steering away from negativity and evil.

> 10 Each heart knows its own bitterness,
>   and no one else can share its joy.

This verse highlights the dignity of emotions, all emotions. That is what makes us who we are. Each person has his or her own heart that has experienced every emotion from bitterness to joy. People should not be judged for their appearance. No one knows what they have been through or have in their hearts.

11 The house of the wicked will be destroyed,
   but the tent of the upright will flourish.

This verse is reminiscent of Proverb 14-1: "The wise woman builds her house, but with her own hands the foolish one tears hers down." The foolish and the wicked, if they are blessed enough to have a house, will do foolish and wicked deeds that will ultimately destroy their homes. They may lose their homes to a fire or foreclosure, or a family member to a drive-by shooting.

The tent, or the house, of the upright, the righteous, and the wise, however, will be prosperous with bounty and family.

12 There is a way that appears to be right,
   but in the end it leads to death.

There are many options to resolving a problem. Many of them are easier than others because they don't require sacrifices or hard work. Most of the time, however, the easy way out is not the right way out. Most of the time, the easy way out requires us to step down the crooked path that leads to death and ruin.

We must take a second look and examine our choices. Are we considering the easy option because it doesn't require us to change our lifestyles or offer moral restraints? Many times, the right choices are hard and require sacrifice. So, let's allow the truth to set us free to make the right choices.

13 Even in laughter the heart may ache,
   and rejoicing may end in grief.

Laughter may mask the heartache of an evil person intent on scheming and deceiving someone. Rejoicing after pulling off an evil scheme most likely will end in grief. So let us not be gullible and fall for the laughter-camouflaged schemes of the evil and wicked person.

14 The faithless will be fully repaid for their ways,
   and the good rewarded for theirs.

The faithless are foolish and unwise. They have no fear of the Lord, as they live wicked lifestyles. They will reap what they sow. Those who do bad things will reap bad consequences. Those who do good things will reap desirable consequences.

15 The simple believe anything,
   but the prudent give thought to their steps.

The simple, or fools, are gullible and have no discernment or good judgment. They trust what they hear without doing the research to find out the truth. Look at all the misinformation presented in the news media.
The prudent, or the wise, however, do not believe what everyone tells them. They are wise and thoughtful about what they believe and plan their future, or their next step.

> 16 The wise fear the LORD and shun evil,
>   but a fool is hotheaded and yet feels secure.

Again, Proverbs 1:7 says, "The fear of the Lord is the beginning of knowledge, but fools despise wisdom and instruction." Fear of the Lord is the foundation of wisdom. Wise people stay away from evil because they know better.

Fools, on the other hand, have no wisdom and fly off the handle at any hint of someone not agreeing with them. They may feel secure because they are too ignorant to know what they don't know or because they are bigger and stronger than their opponent. Physical size and strength, however, will not protect someone from evil. The crooked path of evil still leads fools to death and ruin no matter their physical size.

> 17 A quick-tempered person does foolish things,
>   and the one who devises evil schemes is hated.

Fools are quick-tempered, fly off the handle easily, and do not think through their speech or their actions. So, they say and do stupid things, devise wicked schemes, and are hated because they are evil.

> 18 The simple inherit folly,
>   but the prudent are crowned with knowledge.

The word *folly* means a lack of good sense, or foolishness. The simple, the fools, will inherit foolishness. That is what they are, that is what they know, and that is what they're going to get.

The prudent, or the wise, have knowledge and are always seeking more knowledge. That is what they are, and that is what they do. As a result, they will be rewarded with additional knowledge or wisdom.

> 19 Evildoers will bow down in the presence of the good,
> and the wicked at the gates of the righteous.

Evildoers and the wicked will bow down to the good and righteous people, who will administer justice over them for their evil and wicked acts.

> 20 The poor are shunned even by their neighbors,
> but the rich have many friends.

People want to associate with people they can benefit from. People want to associate with the rich because they have money and hope they can get some of it. It may be in the form of physical currency, or access to parties, illicit drugs, or illicit sex. It may be in the form of access to powerful people to assist in climbing the social or financial ladder.

The sad truth is the poor are shunned even by their neighbors because they not only offer nothing, but they often require effort, time, and money to help them. This is why others shun them. Make the effort to be friends with the poor and help them where you can.

When the money is gone, neither the rich nor the poor have many friends. Rich friends are shallow and hollow, not true friends at all. They are only piranhas, feeding off the rich's wealth.

> 21 It is a sin to despise one's neighbor,
> but blessed is the one who is kind to the needy.

A neighbor is a metaphor for mankind. It is a sin to despise people. Blessings will fall on those who are friends to the poor and kind to the needy.

> 22 Do not those who plot evil go astray?
> But those who plan what is good find love and faithfulness.

Evil and wicked people, who plot evil, are walking on the crooked path, which will lead them to death and ruin. The righteous and wise, who plan, speak, and act out good things will find love and faithfulness. Again, we reap what we sow.

> 23 All hard work brings a profit,
> but mere talk leads only to poverty.

All talk, no game. Know anyone like that? Fools are always bragging about how good they are, but they have no game. That's because game is hard work, and hard work, if done wisely, brings a profit. Talk alone is cheap; it leads only to poverty.

24 The wealth of the wise is their crown,
    but the folly of fools yields folly.

The wealth of the wise is their wisdom, not money. They display their wisdom like a crown. Many of the wise are monetarily wealthy as well because they practice hard work, discipline, saving, and investing. But fools deal in foolishness and end up in foolishness.

25 A truthful witness saves lives,
    but a false witness is deceitful.

Once again, this goes back to the ninth commandment of God: "You shall not give false testimony against your neighbor." Giving false testimony against someone to get them in trouble can get them killed.
Giving a truthful testimony, on the other hand, will save innocent lives from an unjust penalty of death.

26 Whoever fears the LORD has a secure fortress,
    and for their children it will be a refuge.

Having the fear of the Lord means believing in God and following His righteous ways. It means living with wisdom and staying on the straight path. Living this way protects the righteous because they're not involved in wicked and evil situations that will get them harmed or killed. It will be a refuge for their children as well because the wise, who fear the Lord, set an example for their children to follow. Teaching their children in the Lord's ways will create good lives for them, which will be their refuge, a secure fortress.

> 27 The fear of the LORD is a fountain of life,
> turning a person from the snares of death.

The fear of the Lord is the foundation of wisdom because it keeps us on the straight path of righteousness, prosperity, and longevity. We should strive to teach the wicked the fear of the Lord so that they will become wise and to snatch them from the snares of death that reside on the crooked paths.

> 28 A large population is a king's glory,
> but without subjects a prince is ruined.

A king is the leader of his country; he is the government. A king who is a good and righteous leader will do his best to give his people a good life. As a result, the king will have loyal subjects who enjoy and respect the king's leadership and continue to reside in the kingdom.

A king needs all his people to make the kingdom work. He needs the people's tax dollars to have money to operate the government. The people need their king as well. So as long as everyone is fair and respectful, it's a win/win game. But when the king, or the government, abuse their power for their own self-interest, the people become oppressed, overtaxed, and poor. As a result, they are unhappy and move to a better land with a better king or government.

An arrogant king or government may not care about this because they will just tax the remaining people a little more to make up for the shortfall of others moving away. Unfortunately, the kingdom will break down eventually because the overtaxed and oppressed subjects either leave or revolt and overthrow the king. At that point, society collapses and anarchy takes over. Without subjects, the king has no kingdom and is ruined.

> 29 Whoever is patient has great understanding,
>   but one who is quick-tempered displays folly.

As has been discussed repeatedly, fools are arrogant and quick tempered because they are trying to beat down anyone who wants to correct them or give them instruction. The wise are patient and have great understanding because they are also open to instruction or additional wisdom. Anger, however, is appropriate and needed when addressing injustice and sin.

> 30 A heart at peace gives life to the body,
>   but envy rots the bones.

The word *envy* means a feeling of discontented or resentful longing aroused by someone else's possessions, qualities, or luck. Envy rots the bones (eats us up inside) because it's caused by something inside that says "I am inadequate. That person has something I want or possesses some quality that I wish I had. I'm not going to stop until I have it, even if it means making unwise choices." This is also called, keeping up with the Joneses.

Envy is an unwinnable game. There is always someone bigger, stronger, or better looking than we are. There is always someone who has more money, a nicer car, or is better at golf than we are. We need to be happy and content with the lives we have and not long for what others have. We should push ourselves to be better just for the sake of being better, and not to keep up with the Joneses.

> 31 Whoever oppresses the poor shows contempt for their Maker,
> but whoever is kind to the needy honors God.

Everyone on this earth was created by God. In that way, we are all brothers and sisters under God. To oppress and show contempt for the poor is showing contempt for God's children, which is an insult to God's character and design.

Being kind to the needy, on the other hand, is honoring God and all His children.

> 32 When calamity comes, the wicked are brought down,
> but even in death the righteous seek refuge in God.

A *calamity* is a disaster, an event causing great and often sudden damage or distress. When calamity strikes, the wicked are brought down because they are fools that do not plan for potential disasters. Ironically, they often find themselves in precarious situations as a result of the crooked paths they so often walk.

The righteous, on the other hand, find security and confidence in God. Even in the face of inevitable death, they are calmed by their faith in an eternal life with Him.

> 33 Wisdom reposes in the heart of the discerning
> and even among fools she lets herself be known.

The word *reposes* means residing in, situated in, or kept in a particular place. Wisdom resides in the heart of the discerning, those who have good judgment, but even a fool finds a nugget of wisdom every once and a while.

> 34 Righteousness exalts a nation,
> but sin condemns any people.

How healthy and powerful a nation is stems from the righteousness of its government. Is it a good nation? Does it treat the people well or oppress them? Does it feed its people or starve them?

A righteous nation will rise to the top and stay on top. While some nations have great wealth or military might, they cannot sustain a number-one status if they treat their people in an unrighteous manner because their sin will condemn them and they will decay from the inside out.

> 35 A king delights in a wise servant,
> but a shameful servant arouses his fury.

A king or a government is happy with their people who act in a wise and righteous manner, the ones who do everything correctly and do not operate in corruption.

When the people start to act shamefully, however, fury is aroused in the king and the community. Examples of shameful acts are corruption, bribery, or putting their own interests before those of others in the community.

Proverbs 15

1 A gentle answer turns away wrath,
   but a harsh word stirs up anger.

A rising voice and harsh words almost always stir up anger. Gentle words, on the other hand, tend to calm it.

2 The tongue of the wise adorns knowledge,
   but the mouth of the fool gushes folly.

Speech controlled by discipline and sound judgment displays the knowledge of the wise. A fool just runs his or her mouth, highlighting the fact that he or she is a fool.

3 The eyes of the LORD are everywhere,
   keeping watch on the wicked and the good.

The Lord is all knowing and all seeing; He sees both the wicked and the good.

4 The soothing tongue is a tree of life,
    but a perverse tongue crushes the spirit.

A gentle and kind word at the appropriate time can be soothing and healing. The perverse and wicked word, however, crushes one's spirit.

5 A fool spurns a parent's discipline,
    but whoever heeds correction shows prudence.

Disciplining children to teach them how to stay on the straight path and live a right life is so important that it's repeated in Proverbs 3:11-12, 5:23, 10:17, 12:1, and 13:24. Children need to be instructed and disciplined. If they accept the instruction and correction, they will grow to demonstrate prudence and caution.

6 The house of the righteous contains great treasure,
    but the income of the wicked brings ruin.

The righteous are often wealthy because they are wise. They work hard and understand how to save and invest their money to make it grow. More important than money, however, are the fear of the Lord, wisdom, honor, respect, and integrity, which live in the house of the righteous.

Income generated from sinful activities will soon disappear from the wicked person traveling the crooked path to death and ruin.

Proverbs 15

> 7 The lips of the wise spread knowledge,
>   but the hearts of fools are not upright.

An *upright* person is someone who is strictly honorable and honest. The wise speak of and share knowledge.

The hearts, character, or intentions of fools, however, are not upright.

> 8 The LORD detests the sacrifice of the wicked,
>   but the prayer of the upright pleases him.

A *sacrifice* is an act of slaughtering an animal or person or surrendering a possession as an offering to God. A sacrifice was also an act of transferring one's sin to an animal and letting the animal die as repentance for the sin. The Lord dislikes greatly the sacrifice of the wicked because they have no fear of Him. Jesus made the ultimate sacrifice of dying on the cross for the forgiveness of all our sins; no further sacrifice is needed. Prayers of the upright please the Lord because they are many times asking for forgiveness of sin, in lieu of a sacrifice.

> 9 The LORD detests the way of the wicked,
>   but he loves those who pursue righteousness.

The Lord detests the way of the wicked but loves those who pursue righteousness and wisdom. This can also include an ignorant person trying to become wise and learn to do the right thing, or even a wicked person trying to find the fear of the Lord and get on the straight path.

> 10 Stern discipline awaits anyone who leaves the path;
> the one who hates correction will die.

Discipline is also discussed in Proverbs 15:5 among other references. Anyone who leaves the straight path for the crooked path needs discipline to let them know they are not on the straight path and to persuade them to return. The person who hates correction and does not heed the instruction, however, will stay on the crooked path that leads to death and ruin.

Those who choose not to accept instruction and correction are stubborn fools. They carry a chip on their shoulder and are determined to prove to the world that they will do things their way. Such actions will land these people in prison and ultimately kill them.

Let this first piece of wisdom creep into our souls. We need to break down the stubborn walls and accept the fear of the Lord. We need to learn and continue to learn.

> 11 Death and Destruction lie open before the LORD—
> how much more do human hearts!

The Lord is omniscient, which means He is all seeing and all knowing. He sees all death and destruction. He can also see inside our hearts and know our true character. We may be able to put up a front or a façade for others, but the Lord knows the truth.

Proverbs 15   153

> 12 Mockers resent correction,
>   so they avoid the wise.

Mockers, or fools, resent instruction or correction, so they avoid being around wise people who will try to teach them how to improve themselves. Instead they will associate with other mockers and fools and become more foolish. We become like those we associate with, so why not associate with the wise and become wise?

> 13 A happy heart makes the face cheerful,
>   but heartache crushes the spirit.

Happiness brightens our appearance and attitude, which shines out of us. Heartache, on the other hand, makes our hearts hurt (hence the term "heartache") and crushes our spirit. This, too, shines out of us, darkening our appearance and attitude.

> 14 The discerning heart seeks knowledge,
>   but the mouth of a fool feeds on folly.

The discerning heart, the one showing good judgment, seeks knowledge and wisdom. The wise welcome correction and instruction so they can become wiser. Just like we must watch what we eat to stay healthy, we also must watch what we feed our minds. What we allow our minds to consume has an influence on our mental well-being. So, let's not pollute our minds with violent video games, perverse television shows or movies, perverse online videos, or anything that is not helping us grow in a righteous way. A strong desire to discover knowledge is a trait of wisdom.

The fool only consumes foolishness, which includes all the above-mentioned perverse things. As a result, the fool has a polluted mind with alternate realities floating around in it and says and does foolish things. In other words, the fool becomes even more of a fool.

15 All the days of the oppressed are wretched,
    but the cheerful heart has a continual feast.

The word *oppressed* means subject to harsh and authoritarian treatment.

The word *wretched* means of poor quality or very bad.

Totalitarianism is a system of government that is centralized and dictatorial and requires complete subservience to the state.

People who live in oppression, such as slaves or those living under the harsh regime of their government (i.e., those who live under communism or totalitarianism) have bad days, most or all the time because their hearts are constantly full of fear and threat and starve for love, happiness, and good things. The cheerful heart has a continual feast of love with thoughts of the Lord.

If we find ourselves in an oppressed situation, we should not allow fear and dread to get the best of us. Instead we need to allow the Lord to come into our minds and our hearts to feed them with love and happiness. This will change our attitudes and our thoughts.

> 16 Better a little with the fear of the LORD
>   than great wealth with turmoil.

The word *nefarious* means extremely wicked, infamous, or evil. Having great wealth with turmoil refers to ill-gotten wealth acquired by nefarious means such as dealing drugs or blackmail. There often is baggage attached to such wealth. It is better to have a fear of the Lord, which is accompanied by wisdom and righteousness, and have a little wealth than to have great wealth that comes with baggage.

> 17 Better a small serving of vegetables with love
>   than a fattened calf with hatred.

Having a fattened calf for a meal was a luxury reserved for special occasions or for showing opulence. It is better to serve a modest meal with a loving household than to show off by serving an extravagant meal and having a household full of hatred and resentment.

> 18 A hot-tempered person stirs up conflict,
>   but the one who is patient calms a quarrel.

This matter is also mentioned in Proverbs 10:19, 11:12, 12:18. Hot-tempered people run their mouths and cause trouble. Those who are wise, on the other hand, keep their mouths shut, or speak soothing words of healing that calm a situation.

> 19 The way of the sluggard is blocked with thorns,
> but the path of the upright is a highway.

The way of the lazy person is blocked with thorns because they are too lazy to remove them because they are home all day, watching video games and sleeping. The upright, on the other hand, is always busy, working hard for themselves and their families. As a result, their paths are as clear as a well-traveled highway.

> 20 A wise son brings joy to his father,
> but a foolish man despises his mother.

Having a wise son means Mom and Dad raised him to be that way, bringing joy to his mother and father. Raising a son who would grow up to despise his mother, on the other hand, would mean they raised a child who became foolish and wicked.

Maybe Mom and Dad did not discipline their son enough to instruct him in the proper ways. Now they have a foolish and wicked man in their family, who despises his mother, something both parents will be dealing with for the rest of their lives. A little instruction and discipline at a young age can work wonders.

21 Folly brings joy to one who has no sense,
   but whoever has understanding keeps a straight course.

Again is the reference to the straight path that leads to righteousness or the crooked path that leads to death and ruin. Foolishness brings joy to a fool. This often means a detour down a crooked path. Those who have understanding, wisdom, and righteousness, on the other hand, stay on the straight path.

22 Plans fail for lack of counsel,
   but with many advisers they succeed.

Again, fools think they know it all and don't need any help from anyone. They march down what turns to be a wrong path and their plans fail. The wise, however, know what they know, and more importantly, what they do not know. And for that they seek a group of trusted advisors who are knowledgeable of the topic at hand. If someone must go to court, for example, it would be wise for the person to bring a lawyer to represent him or her. If one is building a house, it would be wise to ask an experienced home builder and an engineer for advice. Wise people seek the advice of other wise people, who willingly give or sell their ethical counsel. And for this, their plans succeed.

23 A person finds joy in giving an apt reply—
   and how good is a timely word!

When someone asks you a question, or when you ask someone else a question, it's respectable and responsible to give a reply to the question in a timely manner. Sometimes the reply may take time if it involves research or a task, but the responsible thing to do is let the other person know that you're working on the reply and will have it back to them by a specific date and time and then meet that deadline. This keeps everyone happy.

An untimely reply, on the other hand, makes the asker unhappy and the giver look irresponsible.

> 24 The path of life leads upward for the prudent
>   to keep them from going down to the realm of the dead.

The word *prudent* means acting with or showing care and thought for the future. The straight path leads to fear of the Lord, wisdom, righteousness, and prosperity, while the crooked path leads to death and ruin. The prudent and the wise stay on the straight path, which leads them upward to other straight paths and opportunities. This keeps them from considering going down a crooked path to the realm of the dead.

> 25 The LORD tears down the house of the proud,
>   but he sets the widow's boundary stones in place.

The proud, the arrogant, and the fool will ultimately bring shame and destruction to themselves and their families, who depend on them, by doing something foolish, such as making a bad business deal that causes them to lose their homes and families, or even worse, end up in jail or dead. As a result, their families will find themselves homeless and struggling to survive on their own.

The good news is the Lord helps those who need help. The widow, the wife who has lost her husband, is particularly vulnerable. So, the Lord and the wise people of her community protect and help her so she won't be taken advantage of (i.e., set her boundary stones in place).

In the times of Proverbs, people who owned land would set stones on the property lines or corners to demonstrate where their property was. Crooked, or wicked, neighbors would move the boundary stones to give themselves more property by stealing it from their neighbor.

If the Lord sets your boundary stones in place, they are unmovable. Let the Lord be your boundary stone.

26 The LORD detests the thoughts of the wicked,
    but gracious words are pure in his sight.

The thoughts of the wicked are…well, wicked. The Lord detests wicked thoughts and the wicked people who have such thoughts. Gracious words from a righteous person are received well by the Lord, however; they are pure in His sight because they are in line with the Lord's teachings.

27 The greedy bring ruin to their households,
    but the one who hates bribes will live.

A *bribe* means to act in one's favor, typically illegally or dishonestly, by a gift of money or other inducement. Accepting a bribe as a person of trust and influence to show favor to someone is a serious crime. Examples include a police officer accepting money not to arrest someone, a government official accepting money to make sure a particular company receives a contract for service, a judge accepting money not to prosecute someone of a crime they are guilty of.

People who offer or take bribes are corrupt, dishonest, and greedy. Their acts are major flaws to a fair and honest society. Such people are always found out. And when they are, they will be ruined, disgraced, thrown out of their position, and most likely go to jail. Their homes and families will be ruined.

Bottom line: bribery is a crooked path that leads to death and ruin. Stay far away from it. The one who hates bribes will live.

> 28 The heart of the righteous weighs its answers,
> but the mouth of the wicked gushes evil.

Weighing an answer or words means to pause and think about what we're about to say. It means considering the effects our words will have on a situation, ourselves, or our families.

Fools blurt out the first words that come to their minds. They have "no filter" as we say in our society. Most of the time these words will be evil and have negative consequences.

Proverbs 15

Don't be a fool. Pause and think about your words before you speak them. And know that sometimes nothing at all is the right answer.

29 The LORD is far from the wicked,
   but he hears the prayer of the righteous.

I refer to Proverbs 1:20-33:

Wisdom's Rebuke: Out in the open wisdom calls aloud, she raises her voice in the public square, on top of the wall she cries out, at the city gate she makes her speech. How long will you who are simple love your simple ways? How long will mockers delight in mockery and fools hate knowledge? Repent at my rebuke! Then I will pour out my thoughts to you, I will make known to you my teachings. But since you refuse to listen when I call and no one pays attention when I stretch out my hand, since you disregard all my advice and do not accept my rebuke, I in turn will laugh when disaster strikes you; I will mock when calamity overtakes you-when calamity overtakes you like a storm, when disaster sweeps over you like a whirlwind, when distress and trouble overwhelm you. Then they will call to me but I will not answer; they will look for me but will not find me, since they hated knowledge and did not choose to fear the Lord. Since they would not accept my advice and spurned my rebuke, they will eat the fruit of their ways and be filled with the fruit of their schemes. For the waywardness of the simple will kill them, and the complacency of fools will destroy them; but whoever listens to me will live in safety and be at ease, without fear of harm.

As I have discussed repeatedly, the fear of the Lord is the foundation of wisdom. Wise people humble themselves to the Lord, accept His correction, and embrace His instruction. Because of this, the Lord will make known to them His wise teachings, and He will hear their prayers.

The wicked, on the other hand, have no fear of the Lord and do not accept His rebuke or instruction. The Lord is far away from them and will laugh when disaster strikes them because they did not listen when He called.

> 30 Light in a messenger's eyes brings joy to the heart,
> and good news gives health to the bones.

Obviously, during the time Proverbs was written, there was no internet, tv, or newspapers. Instead, messengers were used to deliver important information, good or bad. Most times the messenger knew the news unless the message was a secret, not to be read by the messenger. When people saw a messenger coming to their home, they knew something big had happened: a new baby had been born, a close relative was sick and near death, a dear friend had been murdered, or an adult child had a terrible accident.

The messenger was tasked with delivering this important news. One look at the messenger's face, and the recipient knew whether the news was good or bad. The light and joy in the messenger's eyes, bringing joy to the

Proverbs 15

hearers, let them know it was good news, which gave them health to their souls and their bodies.

> 31 Whoever heeds life-giving correction
> will be at home among the wise.
> 32 Those who disregard discipline despise themselves,
> but the one who heeds correction gains understanding.
> 33 Wisdom's instruction is to fear the LORD,
> and humility comes before honor.

These three proverbs are working together to repeat an important theme: wisdom. Wisdom is what we're looking for. Wisdom will keep us safe. Wisdom will make us righteous. Wisdom will make us prosperous and happy. Wisdom will bring us honor. To recap, Proverbs 1:7 says "The fear of the Lord is the beginning of knowledge, but fools despise wisdom and instruction." And Proverbs 15:33 says, "Wisdom's instruction is to fear the Lord."

You may be sitting down, reading or listening to this book, and saying to yourself, "I'm trapped in poverty." Or, "I've gotten into trouble down the crooked path a few times, and my life is ruined." Or "I've never read the Bible and I am intimidated by it. I don't know where to start." "I'm only 10 years old; I'm too young to be wise." "I never finished school; how can I be wise?" Or "I'm 75 years old: it's too late for me."

It's never too late to get wisdom. The fear of the Lord is the first step. That means honoring and respecting

God, living in awe of His power, and obeying His Word. These need to be the foundation and controlling principles in our lives, for our understanding of the world, for our attitudes, our speech, and our actions.

Reading this book is a great start. After you finish it, read the Psalms. Many wise people read and pray over the Psalms and Proverbs daily. Don't just read them once and say, "I've read them." Read them every day. That is a good first step to finding the fear of the Lord. Then read the New Testament. I suggest the New International Version (NIV). I also suggest you start with a study Bible that helps explain the verses you are reading.

Then read the Old Testament. It is a challenging read, but stick with it. This will allow you to learn and understand the Lord and His ways, and fear (honor, respect, be in awe of) Him.

The second step to wisdom is to humbly accept discipline and instruction. Don't be an arrogant fool and pretend you know it all, because you don't. Many people with a lot of book knowledge pretend to be wise, but they do not have the fear of the Lord. Ergo, they are not wise.

There are many wise people who never finished high school. Consider the following Proverbs:

- The first half of Proverbs 15:31: "Whoever heeds life-giving correction will be at home among the wise."

- The first half of Proverbs 15:32: "Those who disregard discipline despise themselves," because they will never become wise.

- The second half of Proverbs 15:33 "…and humility comes before honor."

Ok, let's work it backward. Wisdom and honor are our goals. To find wisdom and honor we must have the fear of the Lord. To find the fear of the Lord, we must humble ourselves and have humility.

PROVERBS 16

1 To humans belong the plans of the heart,
 but from the LORD comes the proper answer of the tongue.

The final outcome of the plans we make is in God's hands. We should plan using the tools that God gave us. Our plans should be righteous, just, and good. These are the plans of our hearts. But from the Lord comes the real outcome, which may be in the form of words God puts in our hearts and on our tongues.

2 All a person's ways seem pure to them,
 but motives are weighed by the LORD.

People can talk themselves into pretty much anything, particularly those who have no standard of right and wrong. But the omniscient, all-knowing, Lord knows the motives behind all the decisions a person makes.

3 Commit to the LORD whatever you do,
   and he will establish your plans.

If we truly commit our efforts for the task at hand to the Lord, He will establish our plans for us. But you must trust in God as if everything depends on Him, while working as if everything depends on you.

Another thing to think about is, are your plans for your benefit, or for the Lord's? Some people say that what they are doing is for the Lord, but it's really for themselves. One example might be starting a charity to benefit the poor people in your neighborhood. Are you doing it because you really care about helping the poor? Or are you doing it to pull down a salary and gain notoriety?

4 The LORD works out everything to its proper end—
   even the wicked for a day of disaster.

God has a divine plan; we (even wicked people) are merely pawns in that plan. God will work out every situation to its proper end. The wicked will have their day, which will end up in disaster most of the time. A wicked person's disaster, however, may lead to a righteous person's proper end.

5 The LORD detests all the proud of heart.
   Be sure of this: They will not go unpunished.

Proverbs 16

As mentioned in Proverbs 8:13 and in other places in the Bible, God hates pride and arrogance. Someone thinking they are better than everyone else. Someone thinking they can do everything on their own without assistance from God. Someone who has no fear of the Lord. The proud of heart are really fools, and fools get punished.

> 6 Through love and faithfulness sin is atoned for;
> through the fear of the LORD evil is avoided.

The word *atonement* means reparation for a wrong, or, in this case, sin. Jesus died on the cross to atone for all our sins. Having the fear of the Lord, loving, and having faith in Him, we can repent of our sins and ask God for forgiveness. As stated many times, the fear of the Lord is the foundation of wisdom. Wise and righteous people avoid evil, staying on the straight paths and avoiding the crooked ones.

> 7 When the LORD takes pleasure in anyone's way,
> he causes their enemies to make peace with them.

Do we want the Lord to take pleasure in our way? Of course we do! How do we do that? We start with the fear of the Lord: respect and awe of God and all He has done and created. With this comes wisdom, righteousness, and living a life pleasing to God. When this happens God makes our enemies go away or become peaceful. No enemy wants to fight us when God is with us.

8   Better a little with righteousness
    than much gain with injustice.

Again, another recurring theme, as referenced in Proverbs 15:16. It is better to live a righteous life and be happy with what we have. Evil, greedy, and envious people care more about money and status and will do illegal and unjust acts to get them. And once they have them, they are not satisfied. As a result, many times they will lose them because of the crooked path they took to achieve them.

Some level of financial stability and wealth is necessary to maintain a home, transportation, food, education, etc. But treating wealth as though it were a god that we worship and making it the only thing we care about is not part of a righteous lifestyle.

There are so many very wealthy people that are so very unhappy. They have an empty life because all they care about is money, thinking it will buy them happiness. It proves to be a very hollow goal.

True wealth is being happy, having a happy family, helping and giving to others in need, living a righteous lifestyle. A very rich man once said, "I thought making money was fun until I realized how much more fun it is to give it away."

9   In their hearts humans plan their course,
    but the LORD establishes their steps.

Proverbs 16

This verse is very similar to Proverbs 16:3. The Lord has a divine plan. We must commit our plans to the Lord, and He will establish our steps. We must trust in God as if everything depends on Him, while working as if everything depends on us.

> 10 The lips of a king speak as an oracle,
> and his mouth does not betray justice.

An *oracle* is a priest or priestess acting as a medium through whom advice or prophecy is sought. Kings were thought to be endowed by God with wisdom to establish justice.

> 11 Honest scales and balances belong to the LORD;
> all the weights in the bag are of his making.

This is very similar to Proverbs 11:1, so please refer back to that verse and commentary. Honest scales belong to the Lord because honest scales do not cheat people. The weights in the bag are honest, as well, because they are of His making. Sometimes we may feel we want to cheat a little bit to get that extra profit for ourselves, but God demands honesty in every business transaction. We can't rationalize that we only cheated a little bit because cheating is cheating. Honesty and fairness are not always easy, but they are what God demands. Going out of our way to be fair and honest will gain us a reputation for being upright and just. We can ask God for strength, guidance, and wisdom to be overly honest and fair in our dealings with other people.

12 Kings detest wrongdoing,
    for a throne is established through righteousness.
13 Kings take pleasure in honest lips;
    they value the one who speaks what is right.

As written in Proverbs 16:10, "Kings were thought to be endowed by God with wisdom to establish justice. Their advice and prophecy would not be unjust." Kings often acted as the judges of their kingdoms and punished those who committed crimes. Kings who wished to have a righteous kingdom hated wrongdoing. Lying most often goes along with wrongdoing. The king takes pleasure in those who are honest and speak the truth.

14 A king's wrath is a messenger of death,
    but the wise will appease it.

A king's wrath will come down on those he detests, the wrongdoers described in the last verse. In biblical times, the sentence was often death. When a person is sentenced to death for a crime, even if it was a minor crime, a message is sent for the community to toe the line and don't commit any crimes, because the penalty would be very harsh. The wise lend wisdom, calming words, and a level headedness to the situation that may calm the king and allow the situation to settle down.

15 When a king's face brightens, it means life;
    his favor is like a rain cloud in spring.

Proverbs 16

When a just king's face brightens it means that he is happy. If he is happy, he will spread his favor among his subjects. It means life and prosperity.

> 16 How much better to get wisdom than gold,
> to get insight rather than silver!

As referenced earlier, Proverbs 2:1-5 says, "My son, if you accept my words and store up my commands within you, turn your ear to wisdom and applying your heart to understanding – indeed, if you call out for insight and cry aloud for understanding, and if you look for it as for silver and search for it as for hidden treasure, then you will understand the fear of the Lord and find the knowledge of God."

Wisdom is far more valuable than silver and gold because with it you will understand the fear of the Lord and find the knowledge of God. This is the most important thing we can find because with that knowledge, we can obtain almost anything. Refer back to Proverbs 3:13-18.

> 17 The highway of the upright avoids evil;
> those who guard their ways preserve their lives.

The proverbs often repeat themselves to make sure the lessons are learned. Here again, we have the lesson of the straight path and the crooked path. The upright and righteous people stay on the straight path and avoid evil. Those who guard their ways or make a conscious decision to stay on the straight path preserve their lives. As we know by this point, the crooked path leads to death and ruin.

It's a simple decision really. We can all recognize evil, so if we find ourselves in evil situations with evil people, we need to get out of those situations and away from those people immediately and change direction. We need to think of the wisdom we have gained, get back to the straight path, and preserve our lives.

> 18 Pride goes before destruction,
>   a haughty spirit before a fall.

The word *haughty* means to be arrogantly superior, disdainfully proud, or snobbish. Pride comes before destruction and an arrogant attitude before a fall. Arrogant people are arrogant usually because they are insecure. So, they use their arrogance to make up for their character flaws. They also often refer to themselves in the third person so they don't have to face their weaknesses and stumbling blocks. The old saying comes to mind, "The bigger they are the harder they fall."

Regardless of our level of success, we must maintain a humble spirit. This means knowing all that we have and all that we have accumulated is not ours. Everything we have belongs to God. He's just letting us use it while we're here. So we need to be good stewards of what God has given us or He'll take it away.

Proverbs 16

19 Better to be lowly in spirit along with the oppressed
    than to share plunder with the proud.

In this verse, the proud and arrogant are set aside as not being wise. The wise are not arrogant, they are humble. It is better to be humble in spirit, along with the oppressed, who are also humble in spirit, than to associate with the arrogant and act as they do.

20 Whoever gives heed to instruction prospers,
    and blessed is the one who trusts in the LORD.

This verse illustrates the recurring theme of being open to accepting instruction and correction. Those who are wise are open to instruction because it makes them wiser and they prosper. And remember, the foundation of wisdom is the fear of the Lord. The wise trust in the Lord and are blessed.

21 The wise in heart are called discerning,
    and gracious words promote instruction.

To be *discerning* means having and showing good judgment. The wise have good judgment because they fear the Lord and, as a result, seek and accept instruction.

22 Prudence is a fountain of life to the prudent,
    but folly brings punishment to fools.

Being *prudent* means acting with or showing care and thought for the future. Considering the potential outcomes of our actions (present and future) prolongs the life of the prudent. Not considering the potential outcomes of our actions, is also foolishness or folly, which brings punishment to fools.

The wise, on the other hand, follow God's wisdom, which washes away the effects of sin and ushers in the hope of eternal life with God. This gives us a joyful perspective on life.

> 23 The hearts of the wise make their mouths prudent,
>   and their lips promote instruction.

Again, here we see the combination of instruction and wisdom. The wise give heed to instruction, which means they seek it out and willingly accept it. The hearts of the wise are humble and full of God's wisdom. As a result, the words they speak are prudent and promote further instruction, not only for themselves but also to assist others in becoming wise.

> 24 Gracious words are a honeycomb,
>   sweet to the soul and healing to the bones.

Gracious words are prudent speech because they are kind, humble, and uplifting, meant to be sweet and healing to the people who receive them.

25 There is a way that appears to be right,
   but in the end it leads to death.

God's knowledge is infinite, whereas our knowledge is finite and limited. While we may think we are doing the right thing, we may be unknowingly on a crooked path. That's why we need to trust in God, put our faith in Him, and allow Him to lead us. How do we do this? Through prayer, through asking God to give us strength, guidance, wisdom, and direction to make the proper decision. Once we do this, a direction will appear and become very evident. This may happen immediately or take days, weeks, or months. If it doesn't, we need to stay put, because it's not the direction God wants us to go.

26 The appetite of laborers works for them;
   their hunger drives them on.

Those who are unwilling to work will not eat. Sluggards who are unwilling to put forth the effort to achieve their goals will fail. Those who have a good work ethic are driven to success. They have what is known in today's world as having a "fire in the belly," which means they don't stop until their goals are achieved.

27 A scoundrel plots evil,
   and on their lips it is like a scorching fire.

Evil people plan to do evil things. The words that come out of their mouths are inflammatory, and inflammatory words are an integral part of their evil plot. If we find ourselves in a situation with an evil person, we should remove ourselves from them immediately. No good can come from sticking around.

> 28 A perverse person stirs up conflict,
> and a gossip separates close friends.

People love to gossip because it makes an unimportant person feel important because they know something other people don't. Gossip is most often information about a person that is not flattering. A person's friends often find out this unflattering information because the person confided in someone who told them.

Spreading gossip about someone is a breach of trust. While some people do it because they get a kick out of knowing something someone else doesn't know, others maliciously try to create conflict just to sit back and watch the chaos ensue. This is a perverse and evil act that will certainly cost friendships.

Confidence, which in this case means keeping a secret, is a learned and wise trait because it is a sign of wisdom and professionalism. Gossip, on the other hand, is folly and the work of a fool.

> 29 A violent person entices their neighbor
> and leads them down a path that is not good.

Violent people are evil people, who plan evil things. These may be schemes to steal money or goods, or to plan some sort of revenge. Evil people like someone to share in their evil ways and assure them they are OK. But if we hang out with evil people, they will lead us down a crooked path that leads to death and ruin. Again, it's always best to remove ourselves from such situations immediately.

> 30 Whoever winks with their eye is plotting perversity;
> whoever purses their lips is bent on evil.

Winking is another recurring theme in the proverbs. Refer back to Proverbs 10:10 and the accompanying commentary. Winking is either a sexual come-on or a sign of getting over on someone. It shows this person to be a fool, who has no judgment. Pursing the lips means to pucker, most likely at someone else. This too would fall into the category of plotting perversity and evil. Two acts specifically called out in the Bible thousands of years ago not to do. So let's not do them.

> 31 Gray hair is a crown of splendor;
> it is attained in the way of righteousness.

The crown of gray hair is a mark of old age that is acquired by living a righteous and wise life, walking in the ways of the Lord. God rewards these people with long lives. While young people rejoice in their strength, older people can rejoice in their years of experience and practical wisdom.

32 Better a patient person than a warrior,
   one with self-control than one who takes a city.

A person who can control their temper and anger is stronger than the most powerful warrior given an order to destroy. Self-control is superior to conquest. Losing control and exploding in anger can cost us the very thing we are trying to achieve. This is a good reason for us to learn patience.

33 The lot is cast into the lap,
   but its every decision is from the LORD.

Casting lots in the time of the proverbs was a game of chance used in decision-making. It is similar to flipping a coin or drawing straws today, but casting lots was used to determine God's will. Eventually it became a game that people wagered on, like dice games in a modern-day casino. In Matthew 27:35, Roman soldiers cast lots for Jesus's garments.

The Lord is responsible for every decision, however, not the cast of lots, nor the drawing of the short straw. If we live righteous and humble lives, we will see the Lord making decisions that bring favor on us.

Proverbs 17

1 Better a dry crust with peace and quiet
   than a house full of feasting, with strife.

This verse is similar to Proverbs 15:17. It is far better to have a below-average meal in a righteous, loving, peaceful, and quiet household than feasting in a household filled with hatred and strife.

2 A prudent servant will rule over a disgraceful son
   and will share the inheritance as one of the family.

Children of wealthy and powerful people often feel entitled. They are not prudent, do foolish things, and embarrass themselves and their families. A family will put a prudent, trusted, servant in a position of overseeing a disgraceful child. As a result, the servant earns a better social and economic position in society. The family rewards the servant with a portion, or all, of the disgraced child's inheritance.

3 The crucible for silver and the furnace for gold,
    but the LORD tests the heart.

The crucible and intense heat from the furnace are used to purify silver and gold. So, too, the Lord tests the hearts of His people through trials and diverse circumstances. This is used to purify the hearts of His subjects and teach them to trust in Him. The next time you find yourself in a difficult situation, realize that God wants to use it to refine your faith and purify your heart.

4 A wicked person listens to deceitful lips;
    a liar pays attention to a destructive tongue.

Wicked people associate with other wicked people. They listen to and watch wicked things. They lie back and forth to each other. Wise people, on the other hand, associate with other wise people. They are always seeking knowledge and wisdom and are careful about the material they allow to enter their minds and hearts. It's hard to "un-see" something you've seen. It's hard to "un-remember" something you've allowed yourself to be exposed to. Think of a horror movie you watched that scared you terribly for many nights to come. Don't allow your mind to be polluted with lies and evil things. If you find yourself in this situation, remove yourself from it.

5 Whoever mocks the poor shows contempt for their Maker;
    whoever gloats over disaster will not go unpunished.

God is the creator of all things, which includes all people. Making fun, or mocking, someone is arrogant and foolish. Most of the time this is done by people who are insecure to make themselves look and feel better. Making fun of the weak and the poor is making fun of God's work. Making fun of and gloating over a bad situation almost always comes back to haunt you. The actions of a person tend to decide the fate of his or her future existence.

6 Children's children are a crown to the aged,
   and parents are the pride of their children.

In the times of Proverbs, it was considered a great blessing to live to see one's grandchildren. Parents should be, and in most cases are, the pride of their children. This is assuming they are living a righteous life and acting as good parents, providing for and teaching their children. When we become parents, we stop living for ourselves and start living for our children. Their needs and wants come before ours. We need to be the parents our children would be proud of. Those of us who have parents we are not proud of can use this as an opportunity to break the cycle and not do as they did. Instead, we can be good parents to our children and put them first. In this way, we can be the parents our children will be proud of.

7 Eloquent lips are unsuited to a godless fool—
   how much worse lying lips to a ruler!

A godless fool most likely will not be able to speak wisely and eloquently. Leaders and rulers depend on truth and honesty to administer justice. When leaders are lied to and make unjust decisions, a far greater travesty has been committed.

> 8 A bribe is seen as a charm by the one who gives it;
>   they think success will come at every turn.

Unfortunately, bribery is somewhat prevalent in this world. This means giving money or doing a favor for someone in a decision-making position who can adversely or positively affect an outcome. The person making the bribe thinks, *This is so easy. All I have to do is give them money and I get what I want.* The bribe is the "charm" that gets the results.

Bribery, however, is stealing something that is not yours, and many people go to jail for this crime. Bribery is condemned in the Bible and will come under God's judgment.

> 9 Whoever would foster love covers over an offense,
>   but whoever repeats the matter separates close friends.

To foster love is to promote its growth and development. In a loving relationship, we need to forgive and forget. If one person makes an offense, admits it, and asks for forgiveness, the other person needs to offer forgiveness and forget it. The key point here is forgetting

Proverbs 17

it, which means not mentioning it again. If this person's past offense keeps getting brought up and thrown in his or her face again and again. it will destroy the relationship and the love.

> 10 A rebuke impresses a discerning person
> more than a hundred lashes a fool.

A discerning person shows good judgment and wisdom. A discerning person accepts a rebuke or a reprimand. A person with good judgment and wisdom knows he or she doesn't know everything. If that person did something wrong and got called out for it, the person gladly accepts the criticism and modifies his or her behavior accordingly. A fool, on the other hand, is stubborn, hardheaded, and thinks he or she knows everything. A whipping of a hundred lashes won't change his or her mind.

> 11 Evildoers foster rebellion against God;
> the messenger of death will be sent against them.

Again, to foster is to promote the growth and development of something. Evildoers promote the growth and development of rebellion against God. As a result, God will send the messenger of death against them, most likely on a crooked path.

12 Better to meet a bear robbed of her cubs
   than a fool bent on folly.

Being near a mother bear that has been separated from her cubs is a sure-fire way to get mauled to death by the angry bear. But meeting or associating with a fool bent on folly, or foolishness, is even a more deadly encounter. Again, when we find ourselves in those situations, we need to remove ourselves from them.

13 Evil will never leave the house
   of one who pays back evil for good.

If someone does a good deed for us and we return it with an evil deed, that makes us so wickedly evil that our hearts are turned. In that event, the evil would never leave.

14 Starting a quarrel is like breaching a dam;
   so drop the matter before a dispute breaks out.

Breaching a dam is like going from 0 to 100 very quickly. Starting a quarrel unleashes anger and fury. Restraint, prudence, and discretion should be used to drop the matter, or not bring it up. Avoiding a dam breaching a fury of anger is the action of a wise person.

15 Acquitting the guilty and condemning the innocent—
   the LORD detests them both.

Proverbs 17

The word *corruption* means dishonest or fraudulent conduct by those in power. Leaders who let the guilty go free and convict and condemn the innocent are corrupt. They are wrong and the Lord detests such actions. The aforementioned bribery often plays a role in corruption.

16 Why should fools have money in hand to buy wisdom,
    when they are not able to understand it?

Wisdom cannot be bought. It is achieved first by fear of the Lord and then years of knowledge, learning, and experience. Even if fools could purchase wisdom, they would not be able to comprehend it, because they despise it.

17 A friend loves at all times,
    and a brother is born for a time of adversity.

There is a big difference between being someone's long-time acquittance and being a true friend. True friends are always there for us, in times of struggle and distress. Fair-weather friends, on the other hand, leave the relationship when they are not getting anything out of it. Many true friends refer to each other as brothers or sisters to indicate a bond that cannot be broken. Having a brother or sister with us in a time of adversity means we know they'll always be there for us and will always have our backs.

18 One who has no sense shakes hands in pledge
    and puts up security for a neighbor.

This has been discussed in previous proverbs and is known as co-signing a loan. If someone co-signs a loan for a neighbor, friend, or family member, and that person can't pay it back then the co-signer becomes responsible for repayment. If the co-signer gives the lender collateral, then the lender will take the pledged assets in the event the loan is not repaid. The co-signer almost always has to pay off the loan, destroying relationships with friends or family members. If the borrower cannot qualify for the loan then that person should not have it. Instead of co-signing for a loan, simply give them the money they want to borrow as a gift. You're going to end up without the money one way or the other, so preserve and possibly even enhance the relationship with a gift.

19 Whoever loves a quarrel loves sin;
    whoever builds a high gate invites destruction.

A hot-tempered person commits many sins. Building a high gate or fence invites an attack from a known or unknown enemy. Why would a person have a high fence and gate if there wasn't something valuable in there that may invite an attack?

20 One whose heart is corrupt does not prosper;
    one whose tongue is perverse falls into trouble.

Having a corrupt heart means having an evil heart and being an evil person, constantly speaking perverse and wicked things, which lands them on the crooked path that leads to death and ruin. Obviously, this lifestyle does not lead to prosperity.

21 To have a fool for a child brings grief;
   there is no joy for the parent of a godless fool.

Raising a child who is a godless fool is a burden for the parents, who will be embarrassed by the actions of the child. As a result, they are tasked with bailing the child out of trouble for the rest of his or her life. Unfortunately, it's the fault of the parents for letting their child grow up that way.

The solution is for parents to introduce and induct their children into the fear of the Lord and raising them in a righteous lifestyle of reading the Bible, going to church, and teaching them wisdom. In that way, they can be the parents their children will be proud of.

22 A cheerful heart is good medicine,
   but a crushed spirit dries up the bones.

Our bodies react to what we have in our souls and in our hearts. Being cheerful helps us thrive. Our bodies also react to a spirit that is crushed and full of hopelessness, with nothing left to live for. In that event, our bodies start to shut down until they die. With a loving couple that has been married for decades, for example, if one spouse dies and the other is left alone, the spirit of the surviving spouse is crushed by the loss. There is hopelessness and a wish to be with that departed spouse. As a result, the surviving spouse usually dies of heartbreak and loss soon after.

> 23 The wicked accept bribes in secret
> to pervert the course of justice.

Bribery was mentioned earlier in verse 8 of this proverb. Bribery is a perversion of justice and a serious crime because both the giver and the taker of the bribe are corrupt and evil. Bribes are always transacted in secret, but people usually figure it out. How could this have happened, they ask? Oh…somebody got paid.

The person who accepts a bribe may be an appointed or elected official who serves the public. Refer back to line 15 of this proverb. The Lord detests both acquitting the guilty and condemning the innocent. Maybe one company got a business contract over another because of a bribe. The public gets an inferior product at a higher price, but the decision maker gets paid in secret. Bribery is a corrupt, illegal practice that perverts justice and we should never participate in it in any way.

> 24 A discerning person keeps wisdom in view,
> but a fool's eyes wander to the ends of the earth.

A discerning person has good judgment and wisdom. Goals help us identify and achieve what we want to do in life. It is important to keep our goals in line with God's, so we can be the people He wants us to be: wise, honest, and people of integrity. Prosperity is a good goal, as well.

The fool, on the other hand, has no goals. Their eyes wander to the ends of the earth, chasing wild fantasies, with no thought toward wisdom. When putting together our life goals, we need to put our thoughts toward wisdom. Don't have life goals? Now's the time to make some.

> 25 A foolish son brings grief to his father
> and bitterness to the mother who bore him.

This ties directly to verse 21 of this proverb, so please refer back to that verse and its accompanying commentary.

> 26 If imposing a fine on the innocent is not good,
> surely to flog honest officials is not right.

This verse ties back into verse 15 of this proverb. The Lord detests condemning the innocent. This includes imposing a fine on an innocent person or physically beating a public official. Both are corrupt practices meant to pervert justice.

> 27 The one who has knowledge uses words with restraint,
> and whoever has understanding is even-tempered.

The wise choose their words carefully. Sometimes choosing not to say anything is the correct response. Understanding not to use inflammatory words such as liar, cheater, thief, and whore, keeps a situation and all involved in it even-tempered. This, in turn, keeps a situation from becoming dangerous.

> 28 Even fools are thought wise if they keep silent,
> and discerning if they hold their tongues.

As I have just said in the preceding verse, sometimes choosing not to say anything is the correct response. Even fools sometimes learn. They may not be wise, or know the correct thing to say, but they know enough to keep their mouths shut. And when they do, they don't look foolish, which gets them a little closer to being wise.

PROVERBS 18

1 An unfriendly person pursues selfish ends
 and against all sound judgment starts quarrels.

This is referring to people who only care about themselves. They are often hot-tempered, starting quarrels and using aggression to get what they want. Recognize these people for what they are. They are not wise. Do not associate with them.

2 Fools find no pleasure in understanding
 but delight in airing their own opinions.

Fools blurt out folly because they have no understanding or wisdom, nor do they have any interest in learning or seeking knowledge. All they can do to make themselves feel important is air their own foolish opinions. Don't waste your time with them.

3 When wickedness comes, so does contempt,
   and with shame comes reproach.

The word *contempt* means something that is despised or dishonored. And the word *reproach* means to bring shame upon or to disgrace. Wickedness is despised and brings shame. And with shame comes disgrace. Stay away from wickedness, and stay on the straight path.

4 The words of the mouth are deep waters,
   but the fountain of wisdom is a rushing stream.

Deep waters are unfathomable or inaccessible. So too are the plans and words of people. Such big and unthought out plans may prove to be dangerous. A wise persons' words and wisdom are refreshing and a source of life, like a rushing stream.

5 It is not good to be partial to the wicked
   and so deprive the innocent of justice.

This falls in line with the ninth commandment: "You shall not give false testimony against your neighbor" and with Proverbs 11:1: "The Lord detests dishonest scales, but accurate weights find favor with him." Favoring the wicked and the guilty for any reason deprives justice to the innocent. The Lord detests this, so don't do it or stand for it if you see it.

6 The lips of fools bring them strife,
   and their mouths invite a beating.
7 The mouths of fools are their undoing,
   and their lips are a snare to their very lives.

The word *strife* means a heated or a violent conflict. Fools just run their mouths, accusing people of dumb things, because they have no understanding. This brings them hardship and invites a beating that could turn fatal if the fool says the wrong thing to the wrong person. We need to stay away from fools and avoid being drawn into their conflict. Instead we should just walk away when we hear fools running their mouths about us. In that way, we avoid being brought down to their level of foolishness.

8 The words of a gossip are like choice morsels;
   they go down to the inmost parts.

It's hard not to listen to gossip, just like it's hard not to eat a delicious dessert. Just like a delicious desert never leaves us because it goes straight to the thighs, rear end, or belly, the gossip stays with us, as well. To stay trim, fit, and healthy, we should choose not to eat that delicious dessert and not to listen to gossip. Doing so helps us avoid the cesspool it creates. When a fool says, "Guess what I heard about Joe?" say, "I don't want to hear it" and walk away.

9   One who is slack in his work
    is brother to one who destroys.

One who is slack in his work is lazy, a sluggard. Laziness is one of the causes of poverty and hunger. Poverty and hunger destroy lives. The lazy person is very close to or contributes to the one who destroys lives.

10 The name of the LORD is a fortified tower;
    the righteous run to it and are safe.

Righteous people have a fear of and respect for the Lord. Their faith makes them strong. They ban together and cling to the name of the Lord and are fortified.

11 The wealth of the rich is their fortified city;
    they imagine it a wall too high to scale.

Money comes and money goes. There are too many ways for the rich to lose their wealth. A government may stop backing its currency and it can become worthless overnight. A company goes bankrupt. Someone steals all the money. Inflation robs it of its value.

But God's love never loses its power. He is always dependable. As referenced in Proverbs 18:10, when we become fortified with our faith in God, He will never leave us.

12 Before a downfall the heart is haughty,
    but humility comes before honor.

We heard the message of this verse earlier, so repeating it means it's very important. Proverbs 16:18 says, "Pride goes before destruction, a haughty spirit before a fall." Pride and arrogance come before destruction. The word *haughty* means arrogantly superior, disdainfully proud, or snobbish. An arrogant attitude comes before a fall.

Arrogant people usually have insecurities and use their arrogance to make up for them. They often refer to themselves in the third person. In so doing, they take little account of their weaknesses and do not anticipate stumbling blocks. The bigger they are, the harder they fall, as the saying goes.

Regardless of our level of success, we need to maintain a humble spirit, knowing all we have accumulated is not ours. Everything we have belongs to God. He's just letting us use it while we're here. If we are not good stewards of what God has given us, He'll take it away.

The second half of this proverb is also quoted in Proverbs 15:33, "...and humility comes before honor." Wisdom and honor are our goals. To find wisdom and honor we must have the fear of the Lord. To find the fear of the Lord we must have humility.

13 To answer before listening—
    that is folly and shame.

Proverbs 15:14 says, "The discerning heart seeks knowledge, but the mouth of a fool feeds on folly." When we answer someone before listening it shows we have predetermined the outcome. It shows we have no interest in knowing the other side of the story and that our mind is already made up. Making a sound decision, however, includes seeking all the information, not just the information we currently have. So we should thoughtfully consider the information of others. To do otherwise is to judge without all the facts, which is wrong and shameful.

> 14 The human spirit can endure in sickness,
>   but a crushed spirit who can bear?

This verse is similar to Proverbs 15:13, which says, "A happy heart makes the face cheerful, but heartache crushes the spirit." Our spirit is our soul; it's who we are. A happy or even a normal human spirit has strength enough to endure an illness. A crushed spirit is a spirit of hopelessness, of giving up, of nothing to live for. Those who have a spirit of hopelessness can turn to God, have faith in Him, ask Him to come into your life, and lift your spirit.

> 15 The heart of the discerning acquires knowledge,
>   for the ears of the wise seek it out.

Again, wise people never stop learning. They constantly seek out knowledge. Knowledge gives them understanding and better judgment.

> 16 A gift opens the way
>   and ushers the giver into the presence of the great.

The gift referenced here is a bribe. Great and powerful people, such as a king, are surrounded by their people or their handlers. The handlers control access to the great person. A "gift" to the handler may grant someone access to the king. Kings often dispense favor and judgment to their people. Getting in front of them to ask for a judgment in your favor, or to ask for an opportunity would be very beneficial.

> 17 In a lawsuit the first to speak seems right,
>   until someone comes forward and cross-examines.

Whether hearing a lawsuit in a court of law, or listening to a story in everyday life, it is vitally important to hear both sides before making a judgment, because the first story we hear is the one we tend to believe.

> 18 Casting the lot settles disputes
>   and keeps strong opponents apart.

As referenced in Proverbs 16:33, casting lots is a game of chance used to determine God's will in an irreconcilable situation or dispute. Doing so kept strong opponents from killing each other.

> 19 A brother wronged is more unyielding than a fortified city;
>   disputes are like the barred gates of a citadel.

Back in the time of Proverbs, the eldest son held the birthright and received a larger inheritance than the other sons. Sometimes they would get cheated out of their birthright or sell it, for say, a bowl of soup. A brother wronged or cheated would unleash a fury that would many times lead to the death of the cheater.

> 20 From the fruit of their mouth a person's stomach is filled;
> with the harvest of their lips they are satisfied.

This proverb is similar to Proverbs 12:14. Many people make a living with the words they speak and not with their hands. The wise person speaks wisdom and gains a good harvest from it, like a farmer gains a good harvest from his or her crops.

> 21 The tongue has the power of life and death, and those who love it will eat its fruit.

It is said, "The pen is mightier than the sword." The pen produces words that can be far more dangerous than the physical threat of a sword. The tongue produces words, as well. The words we choose can hold the power of life and death. They have the power to produce wealth, honor, and a long-lasting life. Think of the testimony people give in their own trial. Lawyers are often very good at mastering their words. The one who masters the use of words will eat their fruit.

Proverbs 18

22 He who finds a wife finds what is good
and receives favor from the LORD.

God created marriage between a man and a woman to be joyful and blissful. A married couple is said to become one person. They treat their partner as they would themselves, or even better. They love each other and create a family that will provide love and security for them as they age. They have each other's back 100 percent of the time. Finding a good wife and having a good marriage and family is truly a favor from God.

23 The poor plead for mercy,
but the rich answer harshly.

Unfortunately in life, the rich and arrogant, treat the poor with contempt. These rich and arrogant fools will have to answer to God's judgment.

24 One who has unreliable friends soon comes to ruin,
but there is a friend who sticks closer than a brother.

It's tough being alone. We all need people we can talk to and count on, someone who will be with us during the good times and the bad times. It is better to have one true friend than 100 superficial ones. The best way to find a true friend is to become a true friend to someone.

Proverbs 19

1 Better the poor whose walk is blameless
   than a fool whose lips are perverse.

It is better to live a blameless life and be poor than to live a life of cheating and unlawful practices to gain wealth. The fool whose lips are perverse is the unrighteous person telling lies and despising wisdom to gain wealth.

2 Desire without knowledge is not good—
   how much more will hasty feet miss the way!

The fool or unwise person jumps into things without any planning or knowledge of what they are getting into. The hasty decisions of a greedy or impulsive person chase their reckless desires, meaning they don't think through or research their decisions, or consider the consequences. "…hasty feet miss the way!" means these decisions will turn out to be bad ones.

> 3 A person's own folly leads to their ruin,
>   yet their heart rages against the LORD.

A person's own foolish behavior—pride, arrogance, illegal acts, etc.—will lead to their ruin. And when God punishes these people for their folly, they become angry with God when they should really be angry at themselves.

> 4 Wealth attracts many friends,
>   but even the closest friend of the poor person deserts them.

There are two kinds of friends in this world: 1) A real friend who will be by your side through thick and thin (you might have one or two in this lifetime) and 2) Fake friends, those who want to be around you because you can help them.

When you have wealth, everybody wants to be your friend because they want some of it. Maybe they want to attend one of your lavish parties or ask you to fund their next business venture. They may want a ride on your boat or a stay in your beach house. But these "friends" will disappear fast when you lose your wealth because you don't have anything to offer them anymore. They were never your friends; they just wanted something from you.

> 5 A false witness will not go unpunished,
>   and whoever pours out lies will not go free.

Bearing false witness or testimony against your neighbor is another recurring theme, and is the ninth commandment. Telling lies to get an innocent person condemned for a crime he or she did not commit is illegal. Anyone found out for telling such a lie will find himself/herself convicted of that crime. This person will be in the same jail cell intended for the neighbor.

> 6 Many curry favor with a ruler,
>   and everyone is the friend of one who gives gifts.
> 7 The poor are shunned by all their relatives—
>   how much more do their friends avoid them!
>   Though the poor pursue them with pleading,
>   they are nowhere to be found.

This proverb is similar to Proverbs 19:4. A ruler is wealthy monetarily as well as in a position to offer judgment and favor to his people. As you can imagine, the ruler has many fake friends because he has so much to offer them. The fake friends, however, leave when there is no more wealth or favor to be had.

The poor, on the other hand, have nothing to offer a friend other than loyalty, respect, and friendship. Fake friends and relatives don't care about these things. They only care about themselves and what others can do for them. Find a true friend who will be with you through anything and help you even when you're poor. The way to find a true friend is to become one.

8   The one who gets wisdom loves life;
     the one who cherishes understanding will soon prosper.

Those who find wisdom will love their lives. Why? Because those who are wise live righteous lives filled with good decisions that have been planned. Their family and loved ones support them because that love is reciprocated in a wise fashion. Because they live this way, they will prosper, both monetarily and spiritually. Don't forget Proverbs 1:7: "The fear of the Lord is the beginning of knowledge, but fools despise wisdom and instruction." If fear and faith in God are the foundation and controlling principles in our lives, we will find wisdom.

9   A false witness will not go unpunished,
     and whoever pours out lies will perish.

This is almost a repeat of Proverbs 19:5, so please review that verse and its accompanying commentary. To repeat it in the same proverb and the fact that it is one of the ten commandments shows its level of importance.

10 It is not fitting for a fool to live in luxury—
     how much worse for a slave to rule over princes!

The indentured servant, the slave, does not possess the knowledge or skills to be a ruler. In fact, most likely the slave would be uneducated. Likewise, a fool does not possess the skills or knowledge to appreciate

Proverbs 19

luxury and wealth. As fools do, they will mess it up and lose it all.

> 11 A person's wisdom yields patience;
>   it is to one's glory to overlook an offense.

Wisdom is composed of many good things. Two of them are patience and peace. Overlooking an offense is avoiding conflict. Being patient with someone and not calling them out on every little offense puts us in a ruling position over our offenders. This may help them grow and gain wisdom instead of becoming frustrated and giving up. Helping someone grow and gain wisdom is a glory to a wise person. Wise people love nothing more than helping other people become wise by dispensing and demonstrating wisdom.

> 12 A king's rage is like the roar of a lion,
>   but his favor is like dew on the grass.

A king's rage is both angry and awe inspiring. Both are necessary to rein in insubordinate subjects. His favor is sweet and refreshing like dew on the grass. Life-giving favor.

> 13 A foolish child is a father's ruin,
>   and a quarrelsome wife is like
>   the constant dripping of a leaky roof.

As referenced earlier, having a child who is a fool is a complete embarrassment and many times the downfall of a family. Foolish children come as a result of parents not training and disciplining them so they will grow up with wisdom and instruction to stay on the straight path. Just as a leaky roof wears away at the physical structure of a home, so too does a quarrelsome wife wear away at the structure of the family.

> 14 Houses and wealth are inherited from parents,
>   but a prudent wife is from the LORD.

The word *prudent* means wise in handling practical matters, or using good judgment. Having a prudent wife truly is a gift from God. She is a far better gift than a house or wealth left to us by our parents because she reinforces the fabric and structure of the family.

> 15 Laziness brings on deep sleep,
>   and the shiftless go hungry.

This is similar to Proverbs 6:11 and 10:4. Laziness is the cause of poverty and hunger. Hard work and diligence, on the other hand, bring wealth and prosperity.

> 16 Whoever keeps commandments keeps their life,
>   but whoever shows contempt for their ways will die.

This proverb is referring to the ten commandments as outlined in Exodus 20, which I listed in Proverbs 3 of this book, so please refer to that proverb or Exodus 20 in your Bible. Obeying God's teachings and instructions will cause you to live a righteous and self-preserving life. Not obeying the ten commandments will lead you down a crooked path to death and ruin.

> 17 Whoever is kind to the poor lends to the LORD,
> and he will reward them for what they have done.

God is the creator of all people, rich and poor. Helping the poor is honoring God and His creations. God often uses other people as His tool to help others and accepts the help given to the poor as if we had offered it to Him directly. He will reward this selfless act of kindness.

> 18 Discipline your children, for in that there is hope;
> do not be a willing party to their death.

This verse illustrates another recurring theme about disciplining our children, so refer back to Proverbs 3:11 and 13:24. Our job as parents is to mold and shape our children to do, act, and speak in a righteous and prudent manner so they will stay on the straight path and avoid the crooked path. It's not fun and I'm sure most parents would rather be doing something else. Avoiding this responsibility, however, makes the parents complicit in allowing their children to walk the crooked paths that lead to death and ruin.

19 A hot-tempered person must pay the penalty;
    rescue them, and you will have to do it again.

An angry person uses their anger and violence to control a situation or get their way. This is often illegal and causes the hot-tempered person to be arrested and go to jail. Getting involved in the dysfunctional life of an angry person and trying to rescue them is merely delaying the inevitable. Such involvement, even with good intentions, will most likely cause the rescuer to get caught up in the dysfunctional web of the hot-tempered person's lifestyle. The penalty is discipline (see Proverbs 19:18), which will hopefully make the one who is angry a better person.

20 Listen to advice and accept discipline,
     and at the end you will be counted among the wise.

As referenced numerous times in the proverbs, wise people accept instruction and rebuke or discipline. This is how they become wise and how they become wiser.

21 Many are the plans in a person's heart,
    but it is the LORD's purpose that prevails.

This proverb is very similar to Proverbs 16:1, so please refer back to that proverb and its accompanying commentary.

Proverbs 19 211

22 What a person desires is unfailing love;
    better to be poor than a liar.

Someone who loves us no matter what demonstrates unfailing love. Everyone would love to find a person like that. Honesty is so important in living a righteous lifestyle and being wise. Many people lie to gain wealth, but anything we get from lying is ill-gotten gain. It is better to be poor, honest, and righteous than a wealthy liar.

23 The fear of the LORD leads to life;
    then one rests content, untouched by trouble.

Once again, as is stated so often in Proverbs, the fear of the Lord is the foundation of wisdom because it keeps us on the straight paths, which keep us safe and out of trouble, and off the crooked paths, which lead to death and ruin.

24 A sluggard buries his hand in the dish;
    he will not even bring it back to his mouth!

Sluggards are too lazy to feed themselves. Don't be a sluggard.

25 Flog a mocker, and the simple will learn prudence;
    rebuke the discerning, and they will gain knowledge.

Flogging is a severe form of discipline. A mocker is a simple fool who runs his or her mouth and mocks others. Discipline a mocker and that person will learn good judgment and common sense. Rebuke or correct the ones who already have insight and judgment and they will gain knowledge and become wiser.

26 Whoever robs their father and drives out their mother
is a child who brings shame and disgrace.

In the time of Proverbs, children were responsible for the care and wellbeing of their elderly and sick parents. The children were their parents' main source of security. There were no social security or assisted-living facilities. To disregard this responsibility and cast out one's mother or father would result in great shame and disgrace.

27 Stop listening to instruction, my son,
and you will stray from the words of knowledge.

Listening to a parent's advice helps a child become wise. This helps the child stay on the straight path and avoid the crooked path. If a child stops listening to his or her parents' instruction or heeding their rebuke, the child will stray from the straight path.

28 A corrupt witness mocks at justice,
and the mouth of the wicked gulps down evil.

Proverbs 19

This is referring to a witness who lies to law enforcement or in court. Allowing a lie to guide the outcome of so-called justice makes a mockery of the justice system. The corrupt person who does this is wicked. The wicked love evil and gulp it down like water.

29 Penalties are prepared for mockers,
    and beatings for the backs of fools.

Mockers are fools and fools do stupid things. Fools also rarely learn wisdom and keep repeating their foolish acts. As a result, they get penalized and flogged for them (or go to prison today).

Proverbs 20

1 Wine is a mocker and beer a brawler;
   whoever is led astray by them is not wise.

Wine and beer contain alcohol. Alcohol makes people do foolish things and often become violent. This is true for fools as well as people who are wise. To be led astray by alcohol, however, is not wise, so stay away from it.

2 A king's wrath strikes terror like the roar of a lion;
   those who anger him forfeit their lives.

Back in the times of Proverbs, kings had ultimate power and little patience. They ruled with an iron fist to keep all their subjects in line. To anger the king was a death sentence. We don't have kings today; we have a justice system, but it can still be very harsh. So, we need to respect authority and not anger it. Failing to do so could cost us our freedom and our lives.

3   It is to one's honor to avoid strife,
    but every fool is quick to quarrel.

Those who are wise and confident with their knowledge, understanding, and physical strength have no need to pick a fight because they have no reason to show off their strength. Instead, they will look for a way to avoid the fight. Fools, on the other hand, find it impossible to avoid a quarrel and are always looking for an opportunity to display their folly.

4   Sluggards do not plow in season;
    so at harvest time they look but find nothing.

All of us must use our God-given talents to plan our lives and take action toward making the plan happen. This is similar to preparing a field to plant seeds so that crops will grow. Crops are a form of wealth as they will be harvested and sold or traded for food and goods to sustain the lives of the farmer and his family.

A sluggard, or lazy person, on the other hand, does not have a plan, does not take action, and does not plow the field or plant seeds. So, at harvest time, when everyone else is harvesting their crops and reaping their wealth, the sluggard looks at his field and finds nothing. Who will take care of the sluggard who failed to plan or act? A relative, the church, or the government. Or, perhaps no one.

Make a plan for your life and take action toward fulfilling it.

> 5 The purposes of a person's heart are deep waters,
> but one who has insight draws them out.

This is similar to Proverbs 18:4. Just as deep waters are unfathomable and inaccessible, so are the untold purposes in someone's heart. The wise person with understanding will let his or her good purposes be known and help draw out the untold purposes in others' hearts. This can help establish a plan for their lives and help them take action.

> 6 Many claim to have unfailing love,
> but a faithful person who can find?

Those whose love is unfailing no matter what always support the ones they love and never cheat on them. Finding such unfailing love and loyalty is rare because many people will cut and run when things don't go as planned. So, those who find it should cherish it and offer faithfulness and unfailing love in return. This is truly a gift from God.

> 7 The righteous lead blameless lives;
> blessed are their children after them.

Ever heard the expression, "The apple doesn't fall far from the tree?" Children are always learning and watching their parents. So, parents are teaching their children without even realizing it, and the children will grow up to be what they see. If their parents are righteous and wise, in most cases, their children will be righteous and wise, as well. They will be blessed.

> 8 When a king sits on his throne to judge,
> he winnows out all evil with his eyes.

Kings often sat as judges hearing cases between their subjects. They would not only hear the case, but they would observe the subject's facial expressions and body language, and separate the good from the evil, much like farmers would winnow or separate the wheat from the chaff during the harvest process.

> 9 Who can say, "I have kept my heart pure;
> I am clean and without sin"?

No one can make this statement except the Lord Jesus Christ. We are all sinners and should confess our sins and repent on a regular basis. But even though we repent and ask for forgiveness, evil thoughts and sinful actions move into our minds and body. This is why we need ongoing forgiveness and cleansing.

> 10 Differing weights and differing measures—
> the LORD detests them both.

As outlined in Proverbs 11:1, the Lord upholds moral order, so please refer back to that verse and its accompanying commentary.

Proverbs 20

11 Even small children are known by their actions,
    so is their conduct really pure and upright?

People demonstrate their character through their actions and words. Children, untarnished by the world and all its influences, often say and act in an unbiased and truthful way. Unfortunately, however, the world's negative influences start affecting children from the day they are born.

12 Ears that hear and eyes that see—
    the LORD has made them both.

God made every woman, man, and being on this earth. Ears and eyes are tools God gave us not only to live and survive, but to learn. Wisdom gets into our hearts when we listen to it, watch it, and read it. This is how we become wise.

13 Do not love sleep or you will grow poor;
    stay awake and you will have food to spare.

This refers to being a sluggard or lazy. If we love sleep so much that we do it all the time, we'll be poor because we won't be working. If we stay awake and work, however, we will have enough food and money, with some left over.

> 14 "It's no good, it's no good!" says the buyer—
> then goes off and boasts about the purchase.

This refers to a buyer's deceptive speech when he or she is talking down the quality of an item he or she wishes to buy at a lower price. Once the buyer has succeeded, he or she brags about what a great buy he or she has just negotiated and how it's worth so much more. Wisdom allows us to see through this deceptive speech and not fall for it.

> 15 Gold there is, and rubies in abundance,
> but lips that speak knowledge are a rare jewel.

Wisdom and knowledge are far more valuable than gold and jewels because they allow us to acquire so much more. Finding a wise and righteous person who will share wisdom and knowledge with others is a rare jewel in itself.

> 16 Take the garment of one who puts up security for a stranger;
> hold it in pledge if it is done for an outsider.

This again refers to one person taking responsibility for another person's debt. There are three people involved here:

> 1) the lender: the person giving something to the stranger

2) the borrower: the stranger who needs something

3) the co-signer: the person putting up a valuable garment to be held by the lender in pledge for guaranteeing the repayment of the debt

So many times in these situations the co-signer ends up paying the debt because the borrower defaults on it. This is especially true when the borrower is a stranger with unknown character.

17 Food gained by fraud tastes sweet,
    but one ends up with a mouth full of gravel.

Food, goods, or money obtained by ill-gotten means have no lasting value. Using ill-gotten means to obtain anything is a trip down the crooked path that leads to death and ruin. So, while the initial bite, or windfall, may taste sweet, it will turn as bitter as gall in the end. A mouth full of gravel can mean two things: 1) the sweet food turns to gravel in our mouths, or 2) we find ourselves face down on a gravel road in punishment for our ill-gotten ways.

18 Plans are established by seeking advice;
    so if you wage war, obtain guidance.

This is similar to Proverbs 11:14: "For lack of guidance a nation falls, but victory is won through many advisors." Wise leaders know what they know, but more importantly, they know what they don't know. No one can know everything and be an expert in every field. This is why wise leaders take counsel from many smart advisors, because they may not have all the facts, or their initial instinct may be clouded in bias or misunderstanding. The trick is selecting wise advisors and not biased advisors who will pursue an agenda.

> 19 A gossip betrays a confidence;
>   so avoid anyone who talks too much.

The gossip is mentioned often in Proverbs: 11:13, 16:28, 18:8, and here. A person who gossips causes conflict, breaks up friendships, and betrays another's confidence. This has a way of drawing us into their cesspool of controversy, which they often sit on the sidelines and watch with great joy. People who are known gossips are not trustworthy. They like to stir up controversy because it makes them feel important. It's not worth the headache. If you cannot stay away from the gossip because the person doing the gossiping is a member of your family, do not participate in it. When they come to you and ask, "Want to hear a secret?" just say "no" and walk away.

> 20 If someone curses their father or mother,
>   their lamp will be snuffed out in pitch darkness.

The fifth commandment is "Honor your father and your mother, so that you may live long in the land of the Lord your God is giving you." If we follow the ten commandments, all the wisdom of the proverbs just falls into place. We are to respect our parents even if they don't deserve it. Why? Because guess who's watching us interact with them? That's right, our children. We should be better parents to our children than our parents were to us. This includes breaking the cycle and asking for God's help to become better people. Watching our children grow up to be better than we were is a gift from God.

> 21 An inheritance claimed too soon
>   will not be blessed at the end.

An inheritance is a gift from our parents, grandparents, or another family member. It is meant to make a difference in our lives, a hand up, so to speak. Sometimes it's a small amount of money, and sometimes it's a life-changing amount of money. Sometimes it's a family heirloom, and sometimes it's a piece of land that you and your family can build on.

An inheritance claimed too soon refers to those who receive an inheritance before they become wise or while they are living an unrighteous lifestyle. These people may squander their inheritance on meaningless things. When the money dries up, so do all those "good friends" who latched onto the person who received the inheritance.

A blessed inheritance, on the other hand, is one that

turns into long life, prosperity, generational wealth, success, and power. Wise people plan their estate. Wealth should be left to family with the guidance of a trusted advisor. Parents should not subject young children to a large inheritance they are not ready to handle. They should set up their estates in the form of trusts for the beneficiaries to be released to them over time.

> 22 Do not say, "I'll pay you back for this wrong!"
> Wait for the LORD, and he will avenge you.

It is not our place to take vengeance on others; it's God's. Holding vengeance and hatred in our hearts is a cancer that eats away at our spirits and our bodies. We need to let go of vengeance and have faith that God will establish justice. After all, He has established our judicial system, our world order, and the crooked paths as tools for maintaining justice. The evil people who walk the crooked paths ultimately get what they deserve, death and ruin. We simply need to look forward, not backward, and trust that God has already taken care of the situation.

> 23 The LORD detests differing weights,
> and dishonest scales do not please him.

This was addressed in Proverbs 11:1 and 16:11. It simply boils down to dishonesty, which the Lord hates because it gets into the core of a person. The longer it is there, the harder it is to get rid of. Ultimately, the person gets to a point of not being able to change his or her dishonest ways. This is why we should not lie, not even a little white lie, or cheat, not even a little bit. Instead we should go out of our way to be fair and honest. Go out of your way to be overly fair and honest with others. We also need to confess our sins of dishonesty to God, ask for forgiveness, and then change our ways. We will feel a weight lifted off our shoulders and a new light cast on our lives.

> 24 A person's steps are directed by the LORD.
> How then can anyone understand their own way?

God guides and directs every one of our lives, but we have a hand in making our lives better or worse by the decisions we make. As finite human beings, we have a limited view of where our lives are headed. Only God understands why He puts us where we are and the people we're with. That is why we must put faith in God that He is placing us where we are as part of His overall plan.

> 25 It is a trap to dedicate something rashly
> and only later to consider one's vows.

To *dedicate* means to make a vow or a promise. In religious terms it means making a vow or promise to God in return for an earnest request. God takes vows very seriously. That is why wise and righteous people contemplate any vows or promises made. Trying to go back on a vow can have a very negative outcome.

26 A wise king winnows out the wicked;
 he drives the threshing wheel over them.

This verse is similar to Proverbs 20:8. The threshing wheel pulverizes the grain, separating it from its worthless husk. In the same way, the king, acting as a judge in this case, will separate the wicked from the righteous and administer to the wicked their just punishment.

27 The human spirit is the lamp of the LORD
 that sheds light on one's inmost being.

The human spirit refers to the condition of our hearts. The character, emotions, and spirit inside us make us who we are. Our spirit is the Lord's light within us. Those who are not happy with their spirit need to humbly ask God to give them wisdom, guidance, and the strength to change it.

28 Love and faithfulness keep a king safe;
 through love his throne is made secure.

Love and faithfulness are attributes of God. He puts a king or a ruler in place to help administer order and civilization. A ruler that rules using love and faithfulness is loved by the people he reigns over. They will make his throne secure. Subjects don't love a king who rules using an iron fist and wickedness. At some point they will take matters into their own hands and have their ruler removed by any means necessary.

29 The glory of young men is their strength,
   gray hair the splendor of the old.

Proverbs 16:31 says: "Gray hair is the crown of splendor, it is attained in the way of righteousness." Young men are strong, but they are not wise. Rather, they use their strength and bullheadedness to get their way through life. Gray hair, on the other hand, is the crown of splendor. Those who have gray hair have lived long lives, a reward of the wise.

30 Blows and wounds scrub away evil,
   and beatings purge the inmost being.

Blows, wounds, and beatings refer to harsh punishments inflicted on someone to restrain their evil ways. This has proven to be the most effective method of instilling positive change in someone.

Proverbs 21

1 In the LORD's hand the king's heart is a stream of water
 that he channels toward all who please him.

God has control of the rulers of the earth; He is the one who placed them there. During the time of Proverbs, kings had ultimate authority. God would use them as instruments to assist the righteous and those who pleased Him. Water is a symbol of life.

2 A person may think their own ways are right,
 but the LORD weighs the heart.

It's easy to talk ourselves into a lot of different things, but God looks at the motives in our hearts. Sometimes the right action or choice is difficult to discern. Ask yourself, "Would God be pleased with my action and my motive?" "Am I making a righteous and wise decision that aligns with God's teachings?"

3 To do what is right and just
    is more acceptable to the LORD than sacrifice.

During the times of Proverbs, people would transfer their own sins to a sacrificial animal, and then kill it in the name of God so that He would forgive their sins. The point of this proverb is the Lord would prefer that we not sin at all than to forgive them when we do sin. The best thing to do is what is just and right and avoid the sin.

4 Haughty eyes and a proud heart—
    the unplowed field of the wicked—produce sin.

The word *haughty* means proud or vain to the point of being arrogant. People with an arrogant attitude and heart always feel the need to prove they are better than everyone else. This often leads to wicked acts that produce sin. An unplowed field is begging to be plowed and produce a crop. In this verse, arrogance is the seed, the unplowed field is the garden, and sin is the crop. We should not associate ourselves with the arrogant or try to play their games.

5 The plans of the diligent lead to profit
    as surely as haste leads to poverty.

Wise and diligent people always take time to plan their actions or business moves in writing. Well-thought-out plans of the wise often lead to profit. *Haste* in this verse refers to get-rich-quick schemes, which are not well-thought-out. They are, in fact, hastily made decisions, which lead to losing our money or wealth. This, in turn, leads to poverty.

> 6 A fortune made by a lying tongue
> is a fleeting vapor and a deadly snare.

Evil and wicked people will lie, cheat, and steal to make money. Sometimes they succeed. This falls in line with ill-gotten gains, which we discussed earlier. A fleeting vapor means the fortune will soon disappear. The deadly snare refers to the fact that ill-gotten gains will take the life of those who get them (see Proverbs 1:19). Proverbs 10:2 says, "Ill-gotten treasures have no lasting value, but righteousness delivers from death." And Proverbs 20:17 says, "Food gained by fraud tastes sweet, but one ends up with a mouth full of gravel."

> 7 The violence of the wicked will drag them away,
> for they refuse to do what is right.

The wicked will ultimately become a victim of their own violence because God will bring destruction on those who plunder His people.

> 8 The way of the guilty is devious,
> but the conduct of the innocent is upright.

The conduct of the wicked is devious. The conduct of the righteous and innocent person, on the other hand, is upright.

9 Better to live on a corner of the roof
   than share a house with a quarrelsome wife.

A quarrelsome wife stirs up dissension within the family. During the time of Proverbs, roofs often had flat corners, so small rooms could be built on them.

It's necessary to choose our spouses carefully because we're going to be spending the rest of our lives and bringing children into the world with them. So, it's important to select someone who is beautiful on the inside.

Those who find themselves in a situation with a quarrelsome spouse, get away without leaving the home and breaking up the family. People are often too quick to get divorced. It is not normal. In fact, it is devastating to the children and the couples going through it. That's why it is necessary to find ways to solve problems and keep the family together. One solution is to add a room to the home, providing a place to get away for a brief time.

Those who are quarrelsome spouses need to recognize the destructive behavior and stop it. Those who are not the quarrelsome spouses should consider if their actions and attitudes are the cause of the angry atmosphere in the home. It's necessary for both partners to approach this with wise and humble hearts.

10 The wicked crave evil;
   their neighbors get no mercy from them.

The wicked are devious and crave evil; they have wickedness in their hearts. Unfortunately, their neighbors have to interact with them in some fashion, and sometimes the neighbors' children get swept up in the evil of the wicked. Those who find that their neighbors are evil and wicked should move, or just divorce themselves from the wicked people. Neither they, nor their children, should have any interactions with them and avoid them completely.

11 When a mocker is punished, the simple gain wisdom;
   by paying attention to the wise they get knowledge.

Simple people have little knowledge, but when they see a mocker or a foolish person being punished for doing foolish things, they are able to make the connection between mockery, foolish acts, and punishment. From this association, simple people learn they don't want to be punished, so they had better not become a mocker or do foolish things. They can also learn by taking knowledge from the wise, or by simply observing their ways. Those who want to become wise should find wise people; study their words, actions, and traits; and do what they do. Simple people can also ask them to teach or assist them in becoming wise. If they are truly wise, they will help.

> 12 The Righteous One takes note of the house of the wicked
> and brings the wicked to ruin.

The Righteous One refers to God. God knows who the wicked are, their households, and their hearts. God is the ultimate judge and jury and will bring death and ruin to the wicked.

> 13 Whoever shuts their ears to the cry of the poor
> will also cry out and not be answered.

We should work to help meet the needs of the poor because we may find ourselves in need of assistance one day and appreciate a hand up.

> 14 A gift given in secret soothes anger,
> and a bribe concealed in the cloak pacifies great wrath.

A gift given at the proper time may soothe an angry situation. A bribe hidden from the public, on the other hand, is a circumvention of justice. While it may gain temporary relief from great wrath, it ultimately comes back to destroy all the parties involved in the scandal.

> 15 When justice is done, it brings joy to the righteous
> but terror to evildoers.

Proverbs 21 235

When justice prevails, the righteous rejoice, but it brings terror to the evil and the wicked because they realize they can no longer and avoid justice.

> 16 Whoever strays from the path of prudence
> comes to rest in the company of the dead.

The path of prudence is the earlier-referenced straight path of wisdom, understanding, and righteousness. The other path is the crooked path, the path of evil, wickedness, and folly that leads to death and ruin. Refer back to the Proverbs 7:22-23 and 9:18 encounters with the adulterous woman. Those who have such encounters are straying from the path of prudence.

> 17 Whoever loves pleasure will become poor;
> whoever loves wine and olive oil will never be rich.

God offers us gifts of pleasure and wants us to enjoy them, but this proverb refers to overindulgence in any pleasure. Moderation is OK, but living an excessive lifestyle is not good. Overindulgence in alcohol, drugs, and sex will hinder people's ability to live righteous lives and become successful. In fact, they may become poor and hit rock bottom.

> 18 The wicked become a ransom for the righteous,
> and the unfaithful for the upright.

The wicked and unfaithful people will ultimately experience the wickedness they had intended for the righteous and the upright. Justice will prevail.

> 19 Better to live in a desert
>   than with a quarrelsome and nagging wife.

This verse once again refers to the nagging and quarrelsome wife, so refer back to Proverbs 19:13 and 21:9 and their accompanying commentary.

> 20 The wise store up choice food and olive oil,
>   but fools gulp theirs down.

Wise people live on a budget, don't spend more than they make, don't live in debt, and save for the future or an unseen emergency. Fools, on the other hand, will find themselves broke and in trouble when hard times show up. For those who want to get their financial houses in order, I recommend a book called *The Total Money Makeover* by Dave Ramsey.

> 21 Whoever pursues righteousness and love
>   finds life, prosperity and honor.

The wise pursue righteousness and love, along with knowledge, understanding, justice, and honor. Pursuing these virtues causes them to lead righteous and virtuous lifestyles. Such habits bring with them long lives of prosperity, honor, and happiness.

Proverbs 21

22 One who is wise can go up against the city of the mighty
   and pull down the stronghold in which they trust.

Wisdom is better than strength. Think of the young, strong man who is quick to use his strength in a situation without thinking it through. The wise use their knowledge and understanding to survey a situation and establish a winning plan to defeat the stronghold.

23 Those who guard their mouths and their tongues
   keep themselves from calamity.

The word *calamity* refers to an extraordinarily serious event marked by a terrible loss, lasting distress, and affliction. This is similar to Proverbs 13:3 and 18:21, so please refer back to those verses and their accompanying commentary.

24 The proud and arrogant person—"Mocker" is his name—
   behaves with insolent fury.

The word *insolent* means presumptuous and insulting in manner or speech, arrogant. This verse is similar to Proverbs 3:34, so please refer back to that verse and the accompanying commentary.

25 The craving of a sluggard will be the death of him,
   because his hands refuse to work.

The cravings of the sluggard never end, but he still refuses to even lift a hand to work. He wants something for nothing. This will get the sluggard into wicked schemes that lead down a crooked path. And as we know, crooked paths lead to death and ruin.

26 All day long he craves for more,
    but the righteous give without sparing.

This verse most likely refers to the above-referenced sluggard. All day long the sluggard craves for more but refuses to lift a hand to help himself. The righteous work hard and not only have enough to satisfy themselves and their family's needs, but they have enough to generously give to others. It is necessary to be a good steward of the blessings the Lord has given us. This means not hoarding our blessings, but sharing our wealth to help others.

27 The sacrifice of the wicked is detestable—
    how much more so when brought with evil intent!

God desires His people to be righteous and loving. The sacrifice referred to in this verse is essentially false prayer and devotion. The mindset is "If I go to church, pray, and tithe, God will make me prosperous even though I'm wicked." This is no better than offering God a bribe. God wants our hearts, our complete love and devotion, not religious ritual and volunteer hours.

28 A false witness will perish,
    but a careful listener will testify successfully.

This verse is similar to Proverbs 19:5, so please refer back to that verse and its accompanying commentary.

29 The wicked put up a bold front,
    but the upright give thought to their ways.

The wicked know their lives and their schemes are wicked, even though they put up a bold front to try to hide it. Sometimes they get angry when others question their ways. Reference is made to the adulterous woman in Proverbs 7:13 putting up a bold front to entice the young man down the crooked path of death and ruin. Seduction is one of the hardest pitfalls to run from.

The upright, the ones who live righteous lives, on the other hand, don't walk these crooked paths. They are thoughtful and wise in their actions. They do not make foolish and impulsive decisions. They think through the potential consequences of their actions.

30 There is no wisdom, no insight, no plan
    that can succeed against the LORD.

The Lord has sovereignty and power over His entire creation, and that includes us. There is nothing that we can do, no plan we can overcome, that would succeed against the Lord. Refer back to Proverbs 1:7: "The fear of the Lord is the beginning of knowledge, but fools despise wisdom and instruction." We need to start with a healthy fear and respect for the Lord and let Him direct us to the straight path.

> 31 The horse is made ready for the day of battle,
> but victory rests with the LORD.

The horse is referring to military might. During the time of Proverbs, horses and chariots were supreme weapons against adversaries in battle. Today, our military uses aircraft carriers, fighter jets, and missiles. It is important to prepare for any battle we enter. We can't be a sluggard and not prepare for a battle and think the Lord will always hand us the victory. Our battles may be with illnesses or addictions, but whatever our adversary is, we always need to prepare the best we possibly can, but pray and have faith in the Lord, knowing the victory rests with Him.

Proverbs 22

1 A good name is more desirable than great riches;
to be esteemed is better than silver or gold.

A good name represents a person's character. To have a good name and to be respected is far better than great riches. If you have great riches and a bad name, chances are you received your riches from ill-gotten means. Life is not about money, and anyone who thinks otherwise is a fool. It's about living a good life, being the best person you can be, following God and His teachings, and helping others.

2 Rich and poor have this in common:
The LORD is the Maker of them all.

We are all brothers and sisters under God because He created everyone on this earth. Proverbs 14:31 states: "Whoever oppresses the poor shows contempt for their Maker." To show contempt for the poor is showing contempt for God's people, which is an insult to God's character and design. Being kind to the needy, however, is honoring God and all His people.

> 3 The prudent see danger and take refuge,
> but the simple keep going and pay the penalty.

The wise and prudent are following their plan and always aware of their surroundings. They see danger coming and take prudent actions to avoid it. This may be steering your ship into a safe harbor from a storm or crossing the street to avoid an angry mob. The simple, the fools, on the other hand, are oblivious to their surroundings and keep moving forward. For this they pay the penalty.

> 4 Humility is the fear of the LORD;
> its wages are riches and honor and life.

Proverbs 1:7 says, "The fear of the Lord is the beginning of knowledge, but fools despise wisdom and instruction." Wisdom has many traits, one of which is humility.

The word *humble* denotes meekness and modesty in behavior and attitude, or showing submissive respect. Being humble to the Lord means having a fear and respect for Him. It means demonstrating actions that are righteous in accordance with the Lord's ways. Conducting our lives in such a way will keep us on the straight path. The wages for staying on that path are riches, honor, and a long life.

> 5 In the paths of the wicked are snares and pitfalls,
>   but those who would preserve their life stay far from them.

As stated, many times, the crooked paths of the wicked lead to death and ruin, which in this verse are represented by snares and pitfalls. Staying on the straight path, which is far from the crooked path, is the path of the righteous and the wise. Those who stay on this path are rewarded with a long life.

> 6 Start children off on the way they should go,
>   and even when they are old they will not turn from it.

Read the first few lines of Proverbs 1, 2, 3, 4, and 5. Teach your children good morals and righteous traits while they are young and they will never forget it. Wait too late and the training becomes more difficult. Proverbs 10:13 says: "Wisdom is found on the lips of the discerning, but a rod is for the back of one who has no sense." And Proverbs 13:24 says: "Whoever spares the rod hates their children, but the one who loves their children is careful to discipline them." Proper training early may even limit the use of the rod because they will learn and obey.

> 7 The rich rule over the poor,
>   and the borrower is slave to the lender.

The person who borrows money from someone is a servant to the lender until the loan is repaid, often times with interest so the rich get richer and keep down the poor. The poor are the ones who need the loans the most, but if they take out a loan they cannot afford, with high interest rates, they become a slave to the rich person who is holding their loan. As a result, the loan payments consume the poor and all the money they have.

If they don't have money to repay the loan, they stand to lose everything and, during the time of Proverbs, they may go to debtors' prison. Albert Einstein once said, "Compound interest is the eighth wonder of the world. He who understands it earns it…he who doesn't…pays it." Please remember to check out the book, *The Total Money Makeover*, by Dave Ramsey.

> 8 Whoever sows injustice reaps calamity,
> and the rod they wield in fury will be broken.

The word *sows* means to plant seed by scattering it on or in the earth, or to spread. In the context of this verse, whoever spreads injustice will receive calamity. Those who spread injustice can expect injustice to come back on them. The instrument they use to spread the injustice will be broken.

> 9 The generous will themselves be blessed,
> for they share their food with the poor.

Proverbs 14:21 says, "It is a sin to despise one's neighbor, but blessed is the one who is kind to the needy." Generous people who share their food with the poor will be blessed by the Lord, who considers this a righteous and just act.

> 10 Drive out the mocker, and out goes strife;
> quarrels and insults are ended.

Get rid of the troublemaker (i.e. removing the mocker, or not hanging out with them anymore) and quarrels and strife go away.

> 11 One who loves a pure heart and who speaks with grace
> will have the king for a friend.

Kings, heads of state, and elected officials will show favor to those who have goodness and righteousness in their hearts and who speak with grace. These are characteristics of the wise. Kind people who have such grace and who speak grace make the leader comfortable, so they enjoy being around them and come to depend on them.

> 12 The eyes of the LORD keep watch over knowledge,
> but he frustrates the words of the unfaithful.

In this verse, knowledge refers to people who have knowledge. Having knowledge is more than just being knowledgeable; it includes having a fear of the Lord and following Him. Remember Proverbs 1:7: "The fear of the

Lord is the beginning of knowledge, but fools despise wisdom and instruction." The Lord frustrates the words of the unfaithful.

> 13 The sluggard says, "There's a lion outside!
> I'll be killed in the public square!"

This verse refers to a sluggard, or lazy person, coming up with an excuse not to go to work. Sluggards are ultimately doomed to laziness-induced poverty and trips down the crooked path.

> 14 The mouth of an adulterous woman is a deep pit;
> a man who is under the LORD's wrath falls into it.

The words of an adulterous woman lead to a deep pit that is impossible to get out of. Please refer to Proverbs 5. An unrighteous and wicked man who follows the crooked words (i.e. path) of the adulterous woman may find himself under the Lord's wrath.

> 15 Folly is bound up in the heart of a child,
> but the rod of discipline will drive it far away.

Please refer back to Proverbs 22:6 and its accompanying commentary.

> 16 One who oppresses the poor to increase his wealth
> and one who gives gifts to the rich—both come to poverty.

Proverbs 14:31 says, "Whoever oppresses the poor shows contempt for their Maker, but whoever is kind to the needy honors God." Those who give gifts to the rich want something in return, so this is essentially a bribe. Oppressing the poor and offering bribes (which are illegal and a form of corruption) are detestable in the eyes of the Lord. People who commit these acts clearly love money more than they do the Lord. As a result, the acquired money will be taken from them. The first of the ten commandments says: "You shall have no other gods before me." Loving money more than loving the Lord is a form of idolatry and a breach of the first commandment.

THIRTY SAYINGS OF THE WISE

Saying 1

17 Pay attention and turn your ear to the sayings of the wise;
   apply your heart to what I teach,
18 for it is pleasing when you keep them in your heart
   and have all of them ready on your lips.
19 So that your trust may be in the LORD,
   I teach you today, even you.
20 Have I not written thirty sayings for you,
   sayings of counsel and knowledge,
21 teaching you to be honest and to speak the truth,
   so that you bring back truthful reports
   to those you serve?

Saying 1 of the Thirty Sayings of the Wise is an introduction for the rest of the wise sayings. It is instructing us to keep all the wise sayings in our hearts and have them ready on our lips.

Saying 2

22 Do not exploit the poor because they are poor
    and do not crush the needy in court,
23 for the LORD will take up their case
    and will exact life for life.

These verses are a message of hope to the poor and needy who work under an unjust authoritarian system. It is also a warning to tyrant leaders who rule with an iron fist and offer no mercy. Sometimes God intervenes and destroys them. Some of His favorite ways of doing this are leading an uprising of the oppressed people or having another ruler or country overthrow them. Either way, the tyrant is killed. Those who find themselves in newly placed positions of leadership are not to let their new positions go to their head so that they become tyrants.

Saying 3

24 Do not make friends with a hot-tempered person,
    do not associate with one easily angered,
25 or you may learn their ways
    and get yourself ensnared.

Please refer back to the following proverbs and their accompanying commentaries:

- Proverbs 12:26: "The righteous choose their friends carefully, but the way of the wicked leads them astray."
- Proverbs 13:20: "Walk with the wise and become wise, for a companion of fools suffer harm."
- Proverbs 14:7: "Stay away from a fool, for you will not find knowledge on their lips."

Saying 4

26 Do not be one who shakes hands in pledge
    or puts up security for debts;
27 if you lack the means to pay,
    your very bed will be snatched from under you.

Proverbs 6:1-5 addresses this saying perfectly, so please refer back to those verses and the accompanying commentary.

Saying 5

28 Do not move an ancient boundary stone
    set up by your ancestors.

Please refer back to Proverbs 15:25 and its accompanying commentary.

Saying 6

29 Do you see someone skilled in their work?
   They will serve before kings;
   they will not serve before officials of low rank.

Those who put pride (not arrogant pride) in their work and are hardworking and diligent will become skillful at their craft. Leaders will notice them and want to hire them because they are the best at what they do, and they won't have time to work for lower-ranking officials. A talented painter, for example, will be so busy painting the king's murals and paintings in the palace, he or she won't have time to work for anyone else. So, if we work very hard at our craft and become very skilled, we will be recognized and successful.

PROVERBS 23

Saying 7

1 When you sit to dine with a ruler,
   note well what is before you,
2 and put a knife to your throat
   if you are given to gluttony.
3 Do not crave his delicacies,
   for that food is deceptive.

Sitting down with a powerful leader to dine with is rarely just dinner. You are invited there because he wants something from you. It could be money, influence, or someone to carry out his wicked schemes. By eating his delicacies, you become somewhat obligated to the ruler, because he has now done something for you. As a result, you are pressured to do what the ruler wants, which may lead you down a crooked path. Or, you refuse to do what he wants and... off with your head.

Saying 8

4 Do not wear yourself out to get rich;
   do not trust your own cleverness.
5 Cast but a glance at riches, and they are gone,
   for they will surely sprout wings
   and fly off to the sky like an eagle.

Wise people don't let money be their idol. They don't work themselves to death to get rich. It's very easy to spend money on lavish toys and then it's gone. This is why we should not spend our time chasing fleeting earthly treasures. Instead, wise people store up treasures in heaven that will never be lost. How? By using money to improve the welfare and wellbeing of their family, friends, and neighbors.

Saying 9

6 Do not eat the food of a begrudging host,
   do not crave his delicacies;
7 for he is the kind of person
   who is always thinking about the cost.
   "Eat and drink," he says to you,
   but his heart is not with you.
8 You will vomit up the little you have eaten
   and will have wasted your compliments.

Begrudging hosts are most likely rich people, who are high on the social ladder. They host parties because it is their social obligation. That is how they stay high on the social ladder. The host is not really a friend. He just gets people to attend his party, which is for him. He resents having to do so and resents the cost of the delicacies he has provided. Vomit is the reaction of unwanted guests when they realize they have been used by the begrudging host.

Saying 10

9 Do not speak to fools,
   for they will scorn your prudent words.

Fools despise wisdom and instruction (Proverbs 1:7) hate knowledge (Proverbs 1: 22) and hate correction (Proverbs 12:1). Fools will turn away any prudent words spoken to them, so we should not waste our time and effort.

Saying 11

10 Do not move an ancient boundary stone
   or encroach on the fields of the fatherless,
11 for their Defender is strong;
   he will take up their case against you.

As discussed earlier, moving a boundary stone is stealing someone's property. These verses reference the unprotected or the fatherless. If a man dies and his property is passed on to his young sons, they would be defenseless against a neighbor who wanted to take over some of their land. The defender here could be the redeemer, a family member who would marry the widow out of obligation and take over care of the sons. Or, the defender could be God. Both will take up the case against the property thief.

Saying 12

12 Apply your heart to instruction
 and your ears to words of knowledge.

The wise are always seeking more knowledge in an effort to become wiser. Applying our hearts to instruction means having within our hearts, or our spirits, the want for instruction and knowledge. "And your ears to words of knowledge" means to seek out knowledge wherever we can find it. This may come from listening to an instructor in a class, listening to other wise people, or reading books.

Saying 13

13 Do not withhold discipline from a child;
 if you punish them with the rod, they will not die.
14 Punish them with the rod
 and save them from death.

Disciplining children when they are young gives them a gift of training. Hopefully they learn from it and gain some level of wisdom and understanding. The rod is a reference to beating the child with a rod as punishment. Giving a child this training and understanding helps ensure they won't make foolish mistakes later in life. They won't walk the crooked path that leads to death and ruin. The motivation for this punishment is not anger but forming a godly character in the child.

Saying 14

15 My son, if your heart is wise,
   then my heart will be glad indeed;
16 my inmost being will rejoice
   when your lips speak what is right.

A wise son or child is one who heeds instruction and knowledge. Raising a wise child is the job of the parents. Doing so makes the parents' hearts glad. When the parents watch their child speak and act in a wise manner, their innermost being will rejoice and be proud of the accomplishments of their child and their hard work of raising him or her correctly.

Saying 15

17 Do not let your heart envy sinners,
  but always be zealous for the fear of the LORD.
18 There is surely a future hope for you,
  and your hope will not be cut off.

Proverbs 1:7 says, "The fear of the Lord is the beginning of knowledge, but fools despise wisdom and instruction." Having knowledge and wisdom means having a healthy fear of the Lord. It also means not envying the gains and wealth of the sinners who do not practice God's ways. Their wealth will disappear, and they will have nothing because they do not believe in or follow God's instruction. If we are wise, believe in God, and follow His instruction, He will never leave us. Our hope will not be cut off.

Saying 16

19 Listen, my son, and be wise,
  and set your heart on the right path:
20 Do not join those who drink too much wine
  or gorge themselves on meat,
21 for drunkards and gluttons become poor,
  and drowsiness clothes them in rags.

Proverbs 23

Alcohol, drugs, and gluttony is a crooked path that should never be walked. Addiction to alcohol and drugs will take over people's lives and become all they care about. As a result, they'll ignore their jobs, their families, and all who love them. People who start down this crooked path will become poor, both monetarily and spiritually. It's best not to ever start with alcohol and drugs. Those who have started can stop before it's too late.

Saying 17

22 Listen to your father, who gave you life,
    and do not despise your mother when she is old.
23 Buy the truth and do not sell it—
    wisdom, instruction and insight as well.
24 The father of a righteous child has great joy;
    a man who fathers a wise son rejoices in him.
25 May your father and mother rejoice;
    may she who gave you birth be joyful!

The fifth commandment says, "Honor your father and your mother, so that you may live long in the land of the Lord your God is giving you." We need to listen to the advice our parents give us, respect them, and honor them, even if they don't deserve it. Our children are watching us. It's not too late to establish a new standard of respect and honor.

"Buy the truth" refers to gaining knowledge and wisdom. We must seek out instruction even if we have to buy it. That could be in the form of tuition payments or books.

Children who heed the advice of their parents gain wisdom and grow up to be righteous young adults who bring great joy to their parents. Parents will rejoice in a job well done, raising their child.

Saying 18

26 My son, give me your heart
    and let your eyes delight in my ways,
27 for an adulterous woman is a deep pit,
    and a wayward wife is a narrow well.
28 Like a bandit she lies in wait
    and multiplies the unfaithful among men.

Here the father is pleading with his son to be like him and do as he does. He is teaching his son not to walk the crooked path of the adulterous woman, for she is a deep pit that is inescapable. We discussed the adulterous woman in detail in Proverbs 2:16-19 and 5:1-6, so please refer back to those verses and accompanying commentaries.

The verse "Like a bandit she lays in wait" refers to blackmail. Sometimes in a scheme with her husband, the adulterous woman will lure an unsuspecting victim in, record evidence of the affair, and then blackmail the victim with it. Wealthy men are often the targets. "Pay me, and keep paying me, or I'm going to expose the affair." Lured affairs have cost many people not only their families but their jobs. "…let your eyes delight in my ways," and don't do it.

Saying 19

29 Who has woe? Who has sorrow?
   Who has strife? Who has complaints?
   Who has needless bruises? Who has bloodshot eyes?
30 Those who linger over wine,
   who go to sample bowls of mixed wine.
31 Do not gaze at wine when it is red,
   when it sparkles in the cup,
   when it goes down smoothly!
32 In the end it bites like a snake
   and poisons like a viper.
33 Your eyes will see strange sights,
   and your mind will imagine confusing things.
34 You will be like one sleeping on the high seas,
   lying on top of the rigging.
35 "They hit me," you will say, "but I'm not hurt!
   They beat me, but I don't feel it!
   When will I wake up
   so I can find another drink?"

Who has woe, sorrow, strife, complaints, needless bruises, and bloodshot eyes? The drunkard does. Alcohol and drugs are often used as a crutch to alleviate stress and hardship and quickly become an addiction. When this happens the woe and strife become permanent. Alcoholism and drug addiction will take over a person's life and they will be all that person cares about.

Too much alcohol will dull the senses to a point where the mind becomes confused and the person becomes physically sick, similar to seasickness. Ironically, the person may not feel any pain until the next morning's hangover. At that point, the person will be very sick for the next 24-48 hours. "When will I wake up so I can find another drink?" refers to the addiction pushing the drunkard to get up after a long night of drinking and start drinking again.

Alcoholism and drug addiction are serious traps along a crooked path. Those who have never walked that path should never start. Those who are walking that path need to seek treatment and stop, the same way the wise seek wisdom.

Proverbs 24

Saying 20

1 Do not envy the wicked,
   do not desire their company;
2 for their hearts plot violence,
   and their lips talk about making trouble.

We should not envy the gains and wealth of the sinners, who do not practice God's ways, nor should we desire to be like them. Their wealth will disappear, and they will have nothing because they do not follow God's instruction. They have violence in their hearts and they make trouble wherever they go. Wise people believe in God and follow His instruction. As a result, He never leaves us. Our hope will not be cut off.

Saying 21

3 By wisdom a house is built,
   and through understanding it is established;
4 through knowledge its rooms are filled
   with rare and beautiful treasures.

This is similar to Proverbs 9:1-6. This creates an image of Lady Wisdom and all her benefits coming together in the form of a beautiful home filled with understanding; knowledge; wealth; and, most important, a stable and loving family. It will be a wise household with wise parents who raise wise children.

Saying 22

5 The wise prevail through great power,
   and those who have knowledge muster their strength.
6 Surely you need guidance to wage war,
   and victory is won through many advisers.

Wisdom and knowledge are power. The wise know they cannot be an expert in everything. They may be great leaders and wise in commerce, but they may not be experts in warfare. For the things they are not good at, they retain trusted experts in various fields: "…victory is won through many advisers."

This proverb pertains to warfare, but it also offers wisdom in many other fields. Those in legal situations, for example, need to hire a good lawyer, even if they are lawyers, because it is hard to be objective if they represent themselves. Those who have medical conditions should retain doctors who specialize in the fields that pertain to their illnesses. When we understand what we don't know and check our egos at the door, we win victory in life through many advisers.

Saying 23

7 Wisdom is too high for fools;
    in the assembly at the gate they must not open their mouths.

During the time of Proverbs, the city gate was where the wise leaders met to hold court and resolve disputes. It was also where the city market was. There are fools who are bent on folly just because they are fools and will always be fools. Then there are the young people who make foolish decisions and say foolish things because they have not gained wisdom.

The word *discreet* means having or showing a judicious reserve in one's speech or behavior, or being prudent. The word *discretion* is the act of being discreet.

Fools should not open their mouths and blurt out foolish words that will instigate violence and cause harm to others, but they will, because they are fools. Discretion is a footstep onto the straight path that leads to wisdom.

Saying 24

8 Whoever plots evil
   will be known as a schemer.
9 The schemes of folly are sin,
   and people detest a mocker.

Plotting evil is a sin, just as committing evil is a sin. Mockers are arrogant, loud, insulting, and quarrelsome. Mockers who plot evil and devise evil schemes are sinning when they do so. People detest a mocker and the wickedness they produce.

Saying 25

10 If you falter in a time of trouble,
    how small is your strength!
11 Rescue those being led away to death;
    hold back those staggering toward slaughter.
12 If you say, "But we knew nothing about this,"
    does not he who weighs the heart perceive it?
    Does not he who guards your life know it?
    Will he not repay everyone according to what they
    have done?

The trouble we face today gives us wisdom to face bigger situations in the future. If we wither in this time of trouble and give up, we are destined to be led away to death. Saying, "But we knew nothing about this" leads us staggering toward slaughter. This excuse may be acceptable to ourselves and our weak friends, but not to God. We need to know and have faith in God that He will guard our lives. That gives us the knowledge and strength to accept our challenges head on and fight, knowing that He is training us for something much better. God will repay everyone according to what they have done.

Saying 26

13 Eat honey, my son, for it is good;
   honey from the comb is sweet to your taste.
14 Know also that wisdom is like honey for you:
   If you find it, there is a future hope for you,
   and your hope will not be cut off.

Wisdom is sweet like honey. It is nourishing to the body. When we find honey, we will come back for more because we crave its sweetness and goodness. Wisdom is like honey; once we find it, we will crave it and come back for more. After we consume enough wisdom, we will become wise and make wise decisions, and our hope will not be cut off.

Saying 27

15 Do not lurk like a thief near the house of the righteous,
    do not plunder their dwelling place;
16 for though the righteous fall seven times, they rise again,
    but the wicked stumble when calamity strikes.

God promises to uphold and rescue the righteous. Though they may fall, God will raise them up again. The number seven is used more than 700 times in the Bible. It is used in the context of completeness and perfection, as in seven days a week. It is also used in the context of God's judgment, as in the seven bowls of the Great Tribulation, and the seven seals of God's judgment, in the book of Revelation. The wicked stumble and fall when disaster strikes.

Saying 28

17 Do not gloat when your enemy falls;
    when they stumble, do not let your heart rejoice,
18 or the LORD will see and disapprove
    and turn his wrath away from them.

Gloating is a form of arrogance and pride. Wisdom hates pride. Proverbs 8:13 says, "To fear the Lord is to hate evil; I hate pride and arrogance, evil behavior and perverse speech." The Lord will help us fight our battles, and our victories need to be credited to the Lord. If we take credit for our own victories, gloat, and mock our opponents, the Lord will see and disapprove. And when that happens, He will let us fight our own battles. Be humble and maintain fear and respect for the Lord. Proverbs 16:18 says, "Pride goes before destruction, a haughty spirit before a fall."

Saying 29

19 Do not fret because of evildoers
    or be envious of the wicked,
20 for the evildoer has no future hope,
    and the lamp of the wicked will be snuffed out.

This proverb is almost identical to Psalm 37:1-2, written by King David. King David is King Solomon's father. King Solomon is the author of most of Proverbs. So, King Solomon heeded his father's advice and sought wisdom. King Solomon was known as the wisest man in the world.

We should not give the evildoers any thought. We should not be afraid of them or envy them because the evildoer and the wicked live on the crooked path that leads to death and ruin. They have no hope, and their death is imminent. Instead we are to stay on the straight path.

Saying 30

21 Fear the LORD and the king, my son,
    and do not join with rebellious officials,
22 for those two will send sudden destruction on them,
    and who knows what calamities they can bring?

Fearing the Lord is the foundation of wisdom. This means fearing the king, who represents the civil authority the Lord has put in place. Rebellious officials are people who would attempt to overthrow the king. Committing treason against the Lord or the king will be met with sudden destruction.

FURTHER SAYINGS OF THE WISE

23 These also are sayings of the wise:
    To show partiality in judging is not good:
24 Whoever says to the guilty, "You are innocent,"
    will be cursed by peoples and denounced by nations.
25 But it will go well with those who convict the guilty,
    and rich blessing will come on them.

Showing partiality in judging, or giving the guilty a free pass, is an offense against justice and righteousness. (See Proverbs 18:5.) In this case, the judge will be cursed by the people and lose the respect of other nations. Having a corrupt justice system is a crumbling foundation of a nation soon to fall. Judges who do their jobs and uphold justice by convicting the guilty will receive respect and rich blessings.

> 26 An honest answer
> is like a kiss on the lips.

A kiss on the lips from someone we love is sweet to the soul. So is an honest answer.

> 27 Put your outdoor work in order
> and get your fields ready;
> after that, build your house.

Having crops to feed ourselves (a salary or a cash flow today) and to trade for goods is life sustaining. Building a house is nice and essential; however, it comes at a substantial cost. So, before we take on that cost, we need to have our income established. Then we can build our homes.

> 28 Do not testify against your neighbor without cause—
> would you use your lips to mislead?

The ninth commandment is "You shall not give false testimony against your neighbor." As I have repeatedly referenced, the ten commandments are God's law, which needs to be followed. This proverb dances around "false testimony" and references: "…would you use your lips to mislead?" Telling a lie and giving a misleading statement are both dishonest, pervert justice, and violate the ninth commandment. See Proverbs 24:26.

> 29 Do not say, "I'll do to them as they have done to me;
> I'll pay them back for what they did."

The golden rule as stated in Matthew 7:12 is "So in everything, do to others what you would have them do to you, for this sums up the Law and the Prophets." This quotation is the opposite of the golden rule. It describes revenge, which sadly is the way of this world. Instead of being vengeful, we are to follow the Law and the Prophets and the golden rule.

> 30 I went past the field of a sluggard,
> past the vineyard of someone who has no sense;
> 31 thorns had come up everywhere,
> the ground was covered with weeds,
> and the stone wall was in ruins.
> 32 I applied my heart to what I observed
> and learned a lesson from what I saw:
> 33 A little sleep, a little slumber,
> a little folding of the hands to rest—
> 34 and poverty will come on you like a thief
> and scarcity like an armed man.

These verses describe the dangers of laziness and foolishness. Being a sluggard and a person who has no sense (a fool) are often one and the same. In the times of Proverbs, growing grapes, harvesting them into wine, and selling it was a good way to make a living, but it takes hard work. "A little sleep, a little slumber, a little folding of the hands to rest" means being lazy and not doing the hard work. Instead, the vineyard goes into shambles, no wine is produced, and poverty comes on the vineyard owner like a thief. Not working hard and paying attention to one's business means going broke very quickly.

PROVERBS 25

MORE PROVERBS OF SOLOMON

1 These are more proverbs of Solomon, compiled by the men of Hezekiah king of Judah:

King Hezekiah was a very wise king in the eyes of God. He saw the wisdom in Solomon's proverbs and compiled them to honor King Solomon, for himself, his kingdom, and for all of history.

2 It is the glory of God to conceal a matter;
    to search out a matter is the glory of kings.
3 As the heavens are high and the earth is deep,
    so the hearts of kings are unsearchable.

Humans give God glory because we cannot fully understand His universe. A king gets glory if he can uncover the truth and administer justice. The heights of heaven and the depths of the earth are so vast they are unsearchable, yet God controls the hearts of kings, which He alone can search.

> 4 Remove the dross from the silver,
>   and a silversmith can produce a vessel;
> 5 remove wicked officials from the king's presence,
>   and his throne will be established through righteousness.

Removing the dross from the silver is a purification process. Purified silver is required to create a lasting vessel. A king can produce a lasting and righteous kingdom only after his administration has been purged, or purified, of its wicked officials, who give the king bad advice in an effort to enrich themselves and their families at the cost of the entire kingdom.

> 6 Do not exalt yourself in the king's presence,
>   and do not claim a place among his great men;
> 7 it is better for him to say to you, "Come up here,"
>   than for him to humiliate you before his nobles.

When Jesus noticed how the guests chose to sit at the places of honor at the table, Jesus made a parable of this proverb in Luke 14:7-11: "When someone invites you to a wedding feast, do not take the place of honor, for a person more distinguished than you may have been invited. If so, the host who invited both of you will come and say to you, 'Give this person your

Proverbs 25

seat.' Then, humiliated, you will have to take the least important place. But when you are invited, take the lowest place, so that when your host comes, he will say to you, 'Friend, move up to a better place.' Then you will be honored in the presence of all the guests. For all those who exalt themselves will be humbled, and those who humble themselves will be exalted."

> What you have seen with your eyes
> 8 do not bring hastily to court,
> for what will you do in the end
> if your neighbor puts you to shame?

This verse refers to the seriousness of being in a court and the permanence of the outcome of the case. Those going to court need to prepare their testimonies of their eyewitness accounts with the help of a trusted advisor, a lawyer. Talented lawyers make a living out of twisting people's words and making them look like fools. That is how they win cases.

People may come into court being in the right, with their eyewitness account, but a talented lawyer on the other side can twist their story like a pretzel. This could result in a guilty person getting off or the one who gave the eyewitness account being charged for something he or she did not do. Proverbs 24:6 states " ...and victory is won through many advisors." We should never set foot in a courtroom without being represented by a talented lawyer, no matter how minor the offense.

> 9 If you take your neighbor to court,
>   do not betray another's confidence,
> 10 or the one who hears it may shame you
>   and the charge against you will stand.

These verses give priority to confidentiality over winning a case. The one who hears the case, the judge, may shame a person for breaking his or her oath of confidence and let the charge against that person stand.

> 11 Like apples of gold in settings of silver
>   is a ruling rightly given.
> 12 Like an earring of gold or an ornament of fine gold
>   is the rebuke of a wise judge to a listening ear.

These verses refer to the beauty and value of a carefully crafted court decision that rules correctly. It also refers to the beauty and value of the rebuke of a wise judge regarding a life-giving correction.

> 13 Like a snow-cooled drink at harvest time
>   is a trustworthy messenger to the one who sends him;
>   he refreshes the spirit of his master.

This was addressed in Proverbs 13:17, so please refer back to that verse and its accompanying commentary.

> 14 Like clouds and wind without rain
>   is one who boasts of gifts never given.

Proverbs 25

This verse refers to one who pledges support, most likely to his or her religious institution, and does not honor it. Even worse, this person boasts of his or her pledge to everyone and then does not make it.

Crops are the lifeblood of society because the population lives off them and trades them. They need rain to grow. Clouds and wind get the people's hopes up for rain that never comes. So too is the group relying on the pledge of support that does not get fulfilled. It's very disappointing and could be detrimental to the organization or person relying on the pledge. That's why when we make a pledge, we must honor it and never boast about it. We should just make the pledge, fulfill it, and not discuss it with anyone. That is how wise and honorable people make and fulfill pledges.

> 15 Through patience a ruler can be persuaded,
>   and a gentle tongue can break a bone.

By presenting a ruler with well-thought-out facts and patiently instructing the ruler without pushing, the ruler can be persuaded. "…a gentle tongue can break a bone" is a paradox describing the power of words. Through sensitive and tactful speech, others can be persuaded without violence.

> 16 If you find honey, eat just enough—
>   too much of it, and you will vomit.

17 Seldom set foot in your neighbor's house—
   too much of you, and they will hate you.

Moderation. Too much of anything will make us sick. This includes being at our neighbor's house. If we're invited to go over, then we can go over, but we should be mindful of when to leave, because a proper host will not tell us to leave. Rather, we need to be cognizant of the burden we're placing on the host and not overstay our invitation. If we're invited over to watch a football game, for example, we should leave when the game is over, even if our friend says, "Come on; stay a little longer." They most likely don't mean it; they are just being nice. Most party invitations have starting and concluding times on them. No matter how much fun we're having, when the time for it to conclude comes, we should leave.

18 Like a club or a sword or a sharp arrow
   is one who gives false testimony against a neighbor.

Again, the ninth commandment: "You shall not give false testimony against your neighbor." This is one of the worst things we can do. It is wicked, evil, and against God's law. The emotional pain inflicted on the neighbor is as vicious as an act of physical violence. The next time we're tempted to say something false against someone, we need to imagine ourselves stabbing them with a knife. We are not to give false testimony against anyone.

Proverbs 25

19 Like a broken tooth or a lame foot
    is reliance on the unfaithful in a time of trouble.
20 Like one who takes away a garment on a cold day,
    or like vinegar poured on a wound,
    is one who sings songs to a heavy heart.

These verses are describing the pain and frustration associated with depending on an unreliable person or government, and then listening to their failed excuses.

21 If your enemy is hungry, give him food to eat;
    if he is thirsty, give him water to drink.
22 In doing this, you will heap burning coals on his head,
    and the LORD will reward you.

These verses describe returning good for evil, which the Lord will reward us for. Captured enemies expect to be beaten, tortured, and killed. Showing kindness and giving them life-sustaining food and water will make the uncaptured enemy burn with anger because the captured is being treated better than their own army treats them.

23 Like a north wind that brings unexpected rain
    is a sly tongue—which provokes a horrified look.

In Israel, rain normally comes from the west, not the north. An icy rain coming out of the north would be unexpected, hidden, and dark, and would ruin a farmer's crops. So too is the victim of unexpected slander and gossip, provoking a horrified look.

24 Better to live on a corner of the roof
   than share a house with a quarrelsome wife.

These verses are identical to Proverbs 21:9, so please refer back to that verse and its accompanying commentary.

25 Like cold water to a weary soul
   is good news from a distant land.

These verses highlight the life-giving value of good news.

26 Like a muddied spring or a polluted well
   are the righteous who give way to the wicked.

A spring or a well gives us thoughts of pure, clear, delicious water. So too is the reputation of a righteous person, pure and clear. However, the once-righteous person who compromises his or her values to walk with the wicked has a polluted reputation much like a polluted well or muddied spring. When this happens in the government and in the justice system, the waters of justice are polluted.

27 It is not good to eat too much honey,
   nor is it honorable to search out matters that are too deep.

Moderation in all things is the lesson here, as referenced in Proverbs 25:16. We are mere humans and cannot conceive the vastness that is God and His creation.

28 Like a city whose walls are broken through
    is a person who lacks self-control.

A city with walls that have been broken through is defenseless. A person who lacks self-control is also defenseless because he or she is prone to say and do impulsive and stupid things that will land him or her in trouble or on a crooked path. No one can help this person because he or she is a fool and has no self-control.

Proverbs 26

1 Like snow in summer or rain in harvest,
    honor is not fitting for a fool.

To bestow social respect and honor to a fool could have severe consequences. Like rain in harvest, which could devastate crops, so too could society be hurt by bestowing a position of honor to a fool. Think appointing a foolish person to a powerful position in government as a political favor.

2 Like a fluttering sparrow or a darting swallow,
    an undeserved curse does not come to rest.

An undeserved curse on an innocent person will not come to rest, like a darting swallow. That means that it will have no effect on the innocent person.

3 A whip for the horse, a bridle for the donkey,
    and a rod for the backs of fools!

Simple animals need prodding and instruction in the form of a whip and a bridle to teach them the correct ways. So too is the fool a simple animal that needs discipline (a rod to the back) to control his or her actions and teach him or her the correct ways.

4   Do not answer a fool according to his folly,
     or you yourself will be just like him.
5   Answer a fool according to his folly,
     or he will be wise in his own eyes.

These verses show the contradiction between reason and folly. Some fool's questions are so foolish they do not warrant a response and should be ignored. A fool remains a fool whether he or she is answered or not. Trying to answer a fool's question rationally makes the wise person answering the question stoop to the fool's level. This gives the fool legitimacy and perceived wisdom in his or her own eyes. The wise person has nothing to gain by answering the fool, only something to lose. Wise people, therefore, should ignore fools and their foolish questions.

6   Sending a message by the hands of a fool
     is like cutting off one's feet or drinking poison.

Faithful messengers have a very important and satisfying job for themselves and their patrons. Fools are not meant for any type of serious business, because they are fools. Trusting a fool with an important job will not work out well for anyone. Messengers carried messages that had monumental effects, such as starting a war or executing someone. Trusting a fool for this important job will have a devastating outcome.

> 7 Like the useless legs of one who is lame
>   is a proverb in the mouth of a fool.

A mindlessly quoted proverb from the mouth of a fool is as useless as a paralyzed body part. Proverbs are words of wisdom to be absorbed by those who are receptive to receiving it.

> 8 Like tying a stone in a sling
>   is the giving of honor to a fool.

This is similar to Proverb 26:1, so please refer back to that verse and its accompanying commentary. Like tying a stone in a sling, or putting a bullet into a gun, giving honor to a fool is dangerous.

> 9 Like a thornbush in a drunkard's hand
>   is a proverb in the mouth of a fool.

This verse is similar to Proverb 26:7. A proverb in the mouth of a fool can be as dangerous and irritating as a thornbush in the hands of a drunkard. Proverbs are words of wisdom to be absorbed by those who are receptive to receiving wisdom.

10 Like an archer who wounds at random
   is one who hires a fool or any passer-by.

An archer who wounds at random is someone who causes severe mayhem and death. This is what happens to a person who hires fools or strangers.

11 As a dog returns to its vomit,
   so fools repeat their folly.

Fools repeat their foolish actions, because they never learn. Maybe the rod to the back of the fool will assist in teaching them. Most of the time, however, it doesn't help.

12 Do you see a person wise in their own eyes?
   There is more hope for a fool than for them.

This verse is referring to a person who is arrogant and has a very high self-valuation. Such self-valuation keeps the person from being humble and seeking and gaining wisdom. This delusional condition is worse than that of a fool.

13 A sluggard says, "There's a lion in the road,
   a fierce lion roaming the streets!"

This is similar to Proverbs 22:13, so please refer back to that verse and its accompanying commentary.

> 14 As a door turns on its hinges,
>   so a sluggard turns on his bed.

A sluggard loves to sleep in his bed, never getting up to work. The sluggard will ultimately be doomed from his or her laziness-induced poverty and trips down the crooked path.

> 15 A sluggard buries his hand in the dish;
>   he is too lazy to bring it back to his mouth.

Here sluggards display the height of laziness. They are too lazy to lift their hands to their mouths to feed themselves.

> 16 A sluggard is wiser in his own eyes
>   than seven people who answer discreetly.

Proverbs 26:12 addressed the wiser-in-his-own-eyes problem. A sluggard with a high self-valuation is hard to imagine, but possible. This delusional condition makes the sluggard a fool, as well.

> 17 Like one who grabs a stray dog by the ears
>   is someone who rushes into a quarrel not their own.

If you grab a stray dog by the ears, you get bitten. So too is rushing into a quarrel that is not our own. We're going to get hurt doing that because many times, the two arguing will turn on anyone who is interfering. We should avoid quarrels in general.

> 18 Like a maniac shooting
>   flaming arrows of death
> 19 is one who deceives their neighbor
>   and says, "I was only joking!"

This verse is referring to a troublemaker who inflicts mayhem and tragedy on his or her neighbors and the community. The troublemaker tries to cover it up with the poor excuse of "I was only joking!" This person is clearly a fool and should be avoided at all costs.

> 20 Without wood a fire goes out;
>   without a gossip a quarrel dies down.

Gossips love to create strife and quarrels. They love being in the center of it and then watching it boil over. Without a gossip, the quarrels tend to go away. If you are a gossip, stop gossiping. If you have a gossip in your life, either remove them from your life, or have a talk with them to make them stop gossiping. The latter rarely works and requires many talks and counseling sessions.

> 21 As charcoal to embers and as wood to fire,
>   so is a quarrelsome person for kindling strife.

Similar to the gossip described in Proverbs 26:21, a quarrelsome person likes to quarrel. This person feeds off the chaos created, and many times likes to display his or her physical strength. Many times, a bully will be quick to quarrel to show off his or her strength and fighting ability. Here the advice is simple and clear: we should stay away from quarrelsome people. We shouldn't even be in the same room with them.

> 22 The words of a gossip are like choice morsels;
> they go down to the inmost parts.

The gossip was referenced earlier in Proverbs 18:8, so please refer back to that verse and its accompanying commentary.

> 23 Like a coating of silver dross on earthenware
> are fervent lips with an evil heart.

The word *fervent* means having or showing great emotion or warmth. Silver dross was a cheap substance painted on pottery to make it look different from the clay that it actually was. A coating of dross was meant to dress up and deceive a person of the actual nature of the clay pot. In the same way, a warm and emotional speech will try to hide an evil heart.

> 24 Enemies disguise themselves with their lips,
> but in their hearts they harbor deceit.

Enemies are enemies and they will always remain enemies. Enemies lie and we cannot trust a word that comes from their mouths because in their hearts they harbor deep resentment and deceit against us. They will lie to disguise themselves, but we must never forget that they are our enemies.

> 25 Though their speech is charming, do not believe them,
> for seven abominations fill their hearts.

An *abomination* is an abhorrence or loathing for someone or something. Though our enemies' speech is charming, they are lying. Their hearts are filled with seven abominations, not just one, but seven. This is a loathsome disgust for us, their enemy.

> 26 Their malice may be concealed by deception,
> but their wickedness will be exposed in the assembly.

Malice is a desire to harm others or to see others suffer. The malice of our enemies may be concealed by deception or by their charming speech. But their wickedness will ultimately be exposed in the assembly of God. Proverbs 6:16-19 outlines seven things that are detestable to God: haughty eyes, a lying tongue, hands that shed innocent blood, a heart that devises wicked schemes, feet that are quick to rush into evil, a false witness who pours out lies, and a person who stirs up conflict in the community.

27 Whoever digs a pit will fall into it;
   if someone rolls a stone, it will roll back on them.

Proverbs 1:31 states, "they will eat the fruit of their ways and be filled with the fruit of their schemes." Fools come up with wicked schemes to capture or trap people for gain. This would be to steal from them or to hold them hostage for a ransom. But fools are fools, so they are not very smart. They most often fall victim to the very traps they set for others.

28 A lying tongue hates those it hurts,
   and a flattering mouth works ruin.

As described in Proverbs 26:23-26, our enemies will lie to us because they hold malice and ruin in their hearts for us. Flattery is simply a dressed-up lie meant to make one feel good. This is a method our enemies use to get close to us, breaking down our internal walls by appealing to our egos.

Proverbs 27

1 Do not boast about tomorrow,
    for you do not know what a day may bring.

Only God knows what tomorrow brings. Tomorrow may be a great day, or it could be filled with calamities. We should approach each day with humility before God. We should plan for the worst, but hope and pray for the best.

2 Let someone else praise you, and not your own mouth;
    an outsider, and not your own lips.

Self-praise is arrogant. We should be humble, and not brag about ourselves. If a third party talks about our accomplishments is it more likely to be unbiased.

3 Stone is heavy and sand a burden,
    but a fool's provocation is heavier than both.

Stone and sand are heavy, but heavier is the burden of carrying and ignoring a fool's insults. These insults are meant to engage us and bring us down to the fool's level. We need not take the bait and just ignore the fool's provocation. They are not worthy of a reply. Proverbs 26:4-5 says, "Do not answer a fool according to his folly, or you yourself will be just like him. Answer a fool according to his folly, or he will be wise in his own eyes."

> 4 Anger is cruel and fury overwhelming,
>   but who can stand before jealousy?

Proverbs 6:34 says, "For jealousy arouses a husband's fury, and he will show no mercy when he takes revenge." Jealousy is one of the most powerful emotions there is. It is a level of anger and fury a notch above the average anger and fury. It is not to be messed with. Jealousy is a step on the crooked path that leads to death and ruin. Walking the crooked path of the adulterous woman or the wayward wife ends in the jealous husband leading the "other man" to death and ruin.

> 5 Better is open rebuke
>   than hidden love.

Open rebuke is life-giving correction. Genuine friends will offer each other candid and sometimes harsh advice and concern for the good of the other. If a friend is engaged in a hidden affair with another man's wife, a genuine friend may offer him stern correction to stop before he becomes subject to the jealous husband described in Proverbs 6:34, 27:4.

> 6 Wounds from a friend can be trusted,
> but an enemy multiplies kisses.

Wounds from a friend, open rebukes described in Proverbs 27:5, are genuine and well-directed advice. Kisses, however, cover the intention of harm. Proverbs 5:3-5 says, "For the lips of the adulterous woman drip honey, and her speech is smoother than oil, but in the end she is bitter as gall, sharp as a double-edged sword. Her feet go down to death; her steps lead straight to the grave."

> 7 One who is full loathes honey from the comb,
> but to the hungry even what is bitter tastes sweet.

One who is full is too full to enjoy sweet honey from the comb. This is referring to someone who is too full of folly or error to receive wisdom and instruction. Those who are hungry for wisdom and instruction will take it all in, bitter or sweet.

> 8 Like a bird that flees its nest
> is anyone who flees from home.

Anyone who flees from home too early loses their security and becomes vulnerable to temptation and dangerous schemes of the wicked. This is referring to children running away from home at a young age. This may also be referring to one spouse leaving the other and the household.

> 9 Perfume and incense bring joy to the heart,
> and the pleasantness of a friend
> springs from their heartfelt advice.

Perfume and incense are substances that please the senses. Sincere counsel from a friend also brings joy to the heart.

> 10 Do not forsake your friend or a friend of your family,
> and do not go to your relative's house when disaster strikes you—
> better a neighbor nearby than a relative far away.

Do not fail friends when they are in need. When in need, rely on friendships and not merely family relationships. Our group of friends can be larger and closer than our families. Those who don't have any or many friends can be a friend to someone and make a friend.

> 11 Be wise, my son, and bring joy to my heart;
> then I can answer anyone who treats me with contempt.

Raising a son who is wise brings joy to the hearts of the parents and prevents any accusation against them because it shows they too must be wise. Raising a wise child is the result of a wise and righteous home and lifestyle.

12 The prudent see danger and take refuge,
   but the simple keep going and pay the penalty.

The prudent and wise are always aware of their surroundings and on the lookout for danger. When they see it, they avoid it or take refuge. Fools, on the other hand, are oblivious to their surroundings, so they keep going into the face of danger and don't realize it until it is too late. For this they pay the penalty.

13 Take the garment of one who puts up security for
   a stranger;
   hold it in pledge if it is done for an outsider.

This repeats Proverbs 20:16, so please refer back to that verse and its accompanying commentary.

14 If anyone loudly blesses their neighbor early
   in the morning,
   it will be taken as a curse.

A word delivered in an inappropriate time or an inappropriate manner may be perceived as insincere, hypocritical, or as a curse against a neighbor.

15 A quarrelsome wife is like the dripping
   of a leaky roof in a rainstorm;
16 restraining her is like restraining the wind
   or grasping oil with the hand.

The quarrelsome wife is referenced in Proverbs 19:13 and 21:9, so please refer back to those verses and their accompanying commentaries.

> 17 As iron sharpens iron,
>   so one person sharpens another.

People help others improve themselves. A father and mother teach their children. Teachers educate their students. The wise pass on wisdom to those seeking it. Coaches push their players to the limit and make them the best they can be. Military leaders push their soldiers to the limit and make them the best they can be. It is very fulfilling to be part of iron sharpening iron, regardless of which side we are on. If we're the recipient of the sharpening skills, we have a duty to pass those skills on in our life's journey.

> 18 The one who guards a fig tree will eat its fruit,
>   and whoever protects their master will be honored.

This verse refers to the workers who do the leader's work. The workers who get the job done look out for and protect their leaders. Leaders, in turn, must take care of their loyal employees and let them share in the success of the company. In today's world this is called profit sharing.

> 19 As water reflects the face,
>   so one's life reflects the heart.

One's true character, as it is molded over the years, is reflected in one's heart. We can gain insight into the character of others by observing their conduct, their speech, and how they handle themselves.

20 Death and Destruction are never satisfied,
    and neither are human eyes.

Death and destruction are never satisfied. The wise do what they can to avoid them by living a righteous life and staying on the straight path, but death and destruction always come. The human eye always looks. For some reason, humans cannot avoid looking. When we drive by an automobile accident on the highway, we can't help but slow down and look. It's an insatiable desire to see.

21 The crucible for silver and the furnace for gold,
    but people are tested by their praise.

High temperatures test and purify precious metals. Praise brings an emotion that people like and sometimes seek. People like to be praised for what they do, for doing a good job. People are tested by praise and how they handle it. Does a person work for praise and then relish in it? Or does a person do his or her best all the time and ignore praise? Praise evolves into one's good reputation. It is good to be humble and not relish in praise, but it is also good to have a good reputation and protect it at all costs.

22 Though you grind a fool in a mortar,
    grinding them like grain with a pestle,
    you will not remove their folly from them.

Grinding grain with a mortar and pestle is symbolic of inflicting severe punishment on a fool. Unfortunately, even severe punishment will not remove the foolishness from a fool. Divine intervention is the only help for making a fool a wise person. Those who love a fool or those who do not want to be fools anymore need to seek wisdom.

23 Be sure you know the condition of your flocks,
    give careful attention to your herds;

Proverbs 27:23-27 go together. This verse references a king being aware of the condition of his subjects and servants. In today's world this would refer to a person giving careful attention to and knowing the condition of the people in his or her life: family, employees, friends, etc.

24 for riches do not endure forever,
    and a crown is not secure for all generations.

Money and status are depreciating assets. The wise depend on, but more importantly take care of, the people who take care of them, such as a family and a loving spouse. That also means they take care of their children because they will be the ones taking care of their wise

Proverbs 27

parents when they are old. That also means taking care of trusted employees because without them even those who are wise would not have riches. Proverbs 27:18 references sharing the fruit of our riches with the trusted people that helped us get there. This is a wise thing to do. By promoting the wellbeing of our people, the wise establish their status and secure the method by which their riches are derived.

> 25 When the hay is removed and new growth appears
> and the grass from the hills is gathered in,
> 26 the lambs will provide you with clothing,
> and the goats with the price of a field.
> 27 You will have plenty of goats' milk to feed your family
> and to nourish your female servants.

Livestock, lambs, cows, goats, chickens, and others are self-renewing and increasing sources of means, survival, and wealth, provided by God and harnessed by the wise. Hay is grown in the fields, cut and harvested in the spring and early summer, and used to feed and sustain the livestock during the winter.

Lambs provide not only food but wool that can be used to make clothing. The wool or the clothing can be sold or bartered for other goods.

Goats produce milk. Back in the times of Proverbs, people drank goats' milk at least as much if not more than cows' milk. It provided rich nourishment for people's families and female servants. Goats can also help clear a field in a few weeks because they will eat anything. They also multiply rather quickly. Some of them can be sold or traded for the price of another field for someone's growing empire.

Proverbs 28

1 The wicked flee though no one pursues,
  but the righteous are as bold as a lion.

The wicked do not have a fear of the Lord; they have a fear of other people. The righteous have a fear of the Lord; therefore, they are as bold as a lion and do not fear other people.

2 When a country is rebellious, it has many rulers,
  but a ruler with discernment and knowledge maintains order.

Anarchy means the absence of any form of political authority; it can also mean political disorder and confusion. A stable country is ruled by a person with wisdom and discernment, who will put the good of the country and its people before his or her own selfish wants. When a country is ruled by a selfish leader, anarchy will soon prevail. When anarchy prevails, the leader will be ousted and replaced with another leader. If the new leader is selfish too, the cycle repeats itself.

> 3 A ruler who oppresses the poor
> is like a driving rain that leaves no crops.

Proverbs 14:31 says, "Whoever oppresses the poor shows contempt for their Maker…" A ruler who oppresses the poor is as strong and destructive as a driving rain that leaves no crops and takes the soil away with it. This ruler shows contempt for the Lord and will suffer the Lord's wrath.

> 4 Those who forsake instruction praise the wicked,
> but those who heed it resist them.

Fools forsake, or resist, instruction. They do not wish to know of wisdom or the ten commandments. They do not wish to be schooled in how to act, what to say, or how to work a job that will sustain themselves and their families. They look up to and praise the wicked because they know no better and are impressed by the wicked people's talk and schemes. The wise, who heed instruction, wisdom, and God's law will resist and avoid the wicked.

> 5 Evildoers do not understand what is right,
> but those who seek the LORD understand it fully.

To seek the Lord is to have a fear of and respect for the Lord. Proverbs 1:7 says, "Fear of the Lord is the beginning of knowledge...."

The fear of the Lord is the foundation of wisdom. Those who have a fear of the Lord and those who seek wisdom are following God's law and know what is just and right. Evildoers have no fear of the Lord, are not following God's law, and have no understanding of what is just and right.

6   Better the poor whose walk is blameless
    than the rich whose ways are perverse.

This verse is similar to Proverbs 19:1: "Better the poor whose walk is blameless than a fool whose lips are perverse." These two proverbs are the same except for two words. The words "fool whose lips" were replaced with the words "rich whose ways." You may want to refer back to Proverbs 19:1 and its accompanying commentary.

The difference here is the "fool whose lips" are perverse has now become the "rich [fool] whose ways" are perverse. This is the unrighteous person telling lies and despising wisdom to gain wealth. So, the fool who talked perverse has become rich and now acts perversely.

The interpretation of Proverbs 19:1 still applies: it is better to live a blameless life and be poor than to live an unrighteous life of cheating and unlawful practices to become rich.

> 7   A discerning son heeds instruction,
>   but a companion of gluttons disgraces his father.

Who are the companions of gluttons? Drunkards and sluggards are destined to be lazy and poor. Any of these traits in a son would disgrace a father.

The word *discerning* means showing insight, judgment, perspective, or wisdom. A wise son heeds instruction and makes his parents proud.

> 8   Whoever increases wealth by taking interest or profit from the poor
>   amasses it for another, who will be kind to the poor.

The unjust person works hard at taking advantage of the poor and amassing great wealth. But loaning poor people money and charging them interest is unjust in the eyes of the Lord. The Lord protects the poor and gives back the wealth that was unjustly taken from them.

The Lord will find a way to take the wealth away from the unjust person and give it to someone who will be kind to the poor. How might that happen? Proverbs 5:10 answers this question when talking about the results of an encounter with an adulterous woman: "…lest strangers feast on your wealth and your toil enrich the house of another."

> 9   If anyone turns a deaf ear to my instruction,
>   even their prayers are detestable.

Proverbs 28

God not only hears our prayers, but He clearly hears and knows our intentions. God detests the prayers of someone who prays for forgiveness all the while has the intention of repeating the sin.

> 10 Whoever leads the upright along an evil path
> will fall into their own trap,
> but the blameless will receive a good inheritance.

Proverbs 22:5 says, "In the paths of the wicked are snares and pitfalls, but those who would preserve their life stay far from them."

Proverbs 26:27 says, "Whoever digs a pit will fall into it; if someone rolls a stone, it will roll back on them."

Fools come up with wicked schemes to steal from or hold people hostage for a ransom. Fools being fools, however, they most often fall victim to the very traps they set for others. But the blameless will receive a good inheritance, which is rightfully theirs.

> 11 The rich are wise in their own eyes;
> one who is poor and discerning sees how deluded they are.

The rich think they are wise because they are rich. This is a deluded level of arrogance. Maybe they inherited their wealth. Maybe they are fools who got lucky. Wealth does not equal wisdom, and wisdom does not always bring wealth with it. Many wise people are poor in monetary terms, but rich in wisdom and righteousness. The wise, rich or poor, can see through deluded arrogance.

> 12 When the righteous triumph, there is great elation;
> but when the wicked rise to power, people go into hiding.

Character matters. When a person of great character comes into power, the people will rejoice because their new leader will put the needs and wants of their subjects above his or her own. As a result, the people will prosper, and the community or country will prosper.

The wicked leaders, however, put their own self-interests in front of their people and the community. One way they do this is oppressing the poor, which is addressed in Proverbs 14:31 and 28:3. When the wicked rise to power, good people go into hiding, keeping their heads down, and try to avoid the wickedness.

> 13 Whoever conceals their sins does not prosper,
> but the one who confesses and renounces them finds mercy.

God will forgive us of our sins, no matter how bad the sins are. When we admit and confess our sins to God and renounce them, God will find mercy on us. Whoever conceals their sin and does not repent and ask for forgiveness, however, will not be forgiven and will not prosper.

Proverbs 28

> 14 Blessed is the one who always trembles before God,
>   but whoever hardens their heart falls into trouble.

Again, Proverbs 1:7 says, "The fear of the Lord is the beginning of knowledge, but fools despise wisdom and instruction." The fear of the Lord is the foundation of wisdom. It is respect and reverence for God. Those who fear the Lord will be blessed. Those who do not fear the Lord, who harden their hearts and refuse to let God in, will fall into trouble.

> 15 Like a roaring lion or a charging bear
>   is a wicked ruler over a helpless people.

A wicked ruler feeds on and exploits his or her people like a lion or a bear feed on their prey. This means oppressing helpless people, the poor. Proverbs 14:31, 28:3, and 28:12 all address oppressing the poor. Proverbs 14:31 says, "Whoever oppresses the poor shows contempt for their Maker, but whoever is kind to the needy honors God."

> 16 A tyrannical ruler practices extortion,
>   but one who hates ill-gotten gain will enjoy a long reign.

Tyrannical means having the characteristic of a tyrant or being oppressive.

A tyrannical ruler practices extortion and oppression.

Proverbs 14:31 says, "Whoever oppresses the poor shows contempt for their Maker...."

A tyrannical, selfish ruler who does not put the people's interest first is showing contempt for the Lord and will be met with the Lord's wrath sooner rather than later. Ill-gotten gain is referring to bribes taken for political favors, often used to oppress the poor. Good leaders, who put the interest of their people and country ahead of their own, and who do not take bribes, will enjoy a long reign.

> 17 Anyone tormented by the guilt of murder
> will seek refuge in the grave;
> let no one hold them back.

This proverb references a murderer who is so tormented by a guilty conscience that he or she is contemplating suicide or some form of a death act. Two thoughts here: 1) We are not to get in the way of God's justice, and 2) if the murder feels so guilty, then maybe that person will turn to God for repentance. Either way, let no one keep this person from getting what he or she wants or deserves.

> 18 The one whose walk is blameless is kept safe,
> but the one whose ways are perverse will fall into the pit.

Once again, this is a recurring theme in the book of Proverbs, as it's also in 25:5, 26:27, and 28:10. Fools come up with wicked schemes to steal from people or to hold them hostage for a ransom. Fools being fools, however, they will most often fall victim to the very trap they set for others. But the blameless will be kept safe.

> 19 Those who work their land will have abundant food,
>   but those who chase fantasies will have their fill of poverty.

This is very similar to Proverbs 12:11, so please refer back to that verse and its accompanying commentary.

> 20 A faithful person will be richly blessed,
>   but one eager to get rich will not go unpunished.

A faithful person, who has wisdom and lives a righteous life, will be richly blessed with God's blessings, including wisdom, honor, a loving family, and possibly abundance.

The one who is eager to get rich, however, will be chasing the fantasies described in Proverbs 28:19. This person may receive an inheritance too soon and squander it, taking a trip down a crooked path.

> 21 To show partiality is not good—
>   yet a person will do wrong for a piece of bread.

We live in a very corrupt society. A "piece of bread" is a reference to a small bribe or favor to lure someone into committing a wrongful act of partiality. Showing partiality in return for a bribe is wicked, illegal, and leads to death and ruin.

> 22 The stingy are eager to get rich
>   and are unaware that poverty awaits them.

Proverbs 11:24 says, "One person gives freely, yet gains even more; another withholds unduly, but comes to poverty." Those who are generous with their time, wisdom, and wealth prosper.

The stingy, on the other hand, are only eager to get rich. Poverty awaits them.

> 23 Whoever rebukes a person will in the end gain favor
>   rather than one who has a flattering tongue.

A real friend or loved one will tell us the truth or keep us from doing something we shouldn't. We will eventually realize our friend had our best interest at heart and we will appreciate him or her for the rebuke. This does us far more good than someone who gives us flattering talk to get what he or she wants and doesn't have our best interest at heart.

> 24 Whoever robs their father or mother
>   and says, "It's not wrong,"
>   is partner to one who destroys.

Children are expected to respect their father and mother and take care of them in their old age. This verse refers not only to robbing their parents of monetary goods, but it refers to not giving our father and mother what is owed to them: respect and care. To rob our parents of their possessions as well as the respect and care they deserve will destroy the family.

25 The greedy stir up conflict,
    but those who trust in the LORD will prosper.

The greedy stir up conflict in an effort to get more money. This often doesn't work, however, and gives the person a reputation for being a greedy disrupter. Those who fear the Lord and are wise and generous will prosper.

26 Those who trust in themselves are fools,
    but those who walk in wisdom are kept safe.

Proverbs 3:5-6 says, "Trust in the Lord with all of your heart and lean not on your own understanding: in all your ways submit to him, and he will make your paths straight."

Those who trust in themselves are fools. The fear of the Lord is the beginning of knowledge and the foundation of wisdom. Those who walk in wisdom are kept safe because they are wise. Wisdom keeps them from the crooked path that leads to death and ruin.

27 Those who give to the poor will lack nothing,
   but those who close their eyes to them receive many curses.

This verse is similar to Proverbs 11:24: "One person gives freely, yet gains even more; another withholds unduly, but comes to poverty." Those who close their eyes to the poor and are not generous will receive many curses, which will most likely include poverty, the same plight as the poor.

28 When the wicked rise to power, people go into hiding;
   but when the wicked perish, the righteous thrive.

This is similar to Proverbs 28:12, so please refer back to that verse and its accompanying commentary.

Proverbs 29

1 Whoever remains stiff-necked after many rebukes
will suddenly be destroyed—without remedy.

This is referring to those who defy authority again and again and do not side with the righteous. This is a stiff-necked fool, who is beyond cure and will find himself or herself on a crooked path leading to death and ruin.

2 When the righteous thrive, the people rejoice;
when the wicked rule, the people groan.

The righteous thrive and rejoice when they have a good leader who puts their needs before their own. Wicked rulers, on the other hand, oppress the people and the poor, and the people groan.

3 A man who loves wisdom brings joy to his father,
but a companion of prostitutes squanders his wealth.

Raising a son who is wise brings great joy to a mother and a father because they know they have succeeded in their most important job, raising a good child. The second half of this verse refers to this same man who had a lapse in judgment and spent time with prostitutes. Succumbing to lust is a great way for people to lose all of their wealth. When mixed with adultery, it is a great way for people to lose their lives and all their belongings.

> 4 By justice a king gives a country stability,
> but those who are greedy for bribes tear it down.

A wise and just king puts the needs of his people before his own and gives a country stability. The greedy and unjust king, on the other hand, puts his own needs before those of his people. He accepts bribes to enrich himself, allowing special interest to rule and pillage the country, causing great instability.

> 5 Those who flatter their neighbors
> are spreading nets for their feet.

Those who flatter their neighbors are trying to get something from them or trap them in a scheme. Fools who set traps for others most always become victims of their own work.

> 6 Evildoers are snared by their own sin,
> but the righteous shout for joy and are glad.

As referenced in Proverbs 29:5, fools are snared by their own sin. They become victims of the very trap they have set for others or some consequence resulting from it.

The righteous, on the other hand, are wise and have a fear of the Lord. As a result, they stay on the straight path, and the Lord offers them happiness and prosperity. They shout for joy and are glad.

> 7 The righteous care about justice for the poor,
> but the wicked have no such concern.

A defining feature of righteousness reflects God's concern for the poor. The poor are often oppressed because they have no knowledge or means to fight an unjust society. The wicked are often the oppressors and have no such concern. Righteous people care about justice for all.

> 8 Mockers stir up a city,
> but the wise turn away anger.

The wise avoid or walk away from an angry situation because they know that no good will come from it. Mockers, or fools, by contrast, enjoy controversy and mayhem.

> 9 If a wise person goes to court with a fool,
> the fool rages and scoffs, and there is no peace.

The fool refuses to listen to reason and instead causes a commotion. There is no peace because the judge will not put up with it. If we go to court with fools, we may get sentenced right along with them, so it's best never to associate with them.

Say, for example, you decide to hang out with a fool. You're driving your car and the fool is in the front seat. He says, "Hey, I'm thirsty; stop at this gas station so I can buy a soda."

"Sure," you say.

Three minutes later the fool comes running out of the gas station with a gun in one hand, a fist full of money in the other hand, jumps into the front seat, and says "drive." Now what do you do? You're up to your neck in an armed robbery.

That's why we shouldn't allow fools to bring us in on their folly.

> 10 The bloodthirsty hate a person of integrity
>   and seek to kill the upright.

Proverbs 1:11-16 gives an outline of why sinful men entice. Wicked, evil, and bloodthirsty people have no integrity and hate people who do. Because of this, they seek to kill those with integrity to make themselves feel better, to get all sorts of valuable things, and fill their houses with plunder.

> 11 Fools give full vent to their rage,
>   but the wise bring calm in the end.

Proverbs 29 319

Proverbs 14:16-17 says, "The wise fear the Lord and shun evil, but a fool is hotheaded and yet feels secure. A quick-tempered person does foolish things, and the one who devises evil schemes is hated." The theme of Proverbs 29 is "the wise avoid anger." Fools enjoy stirring up trouble, so we need to stay away from them because we may get wrapped up in their mayhem.

12 If a ruler listens to lies,
    all his officials become wicked.

Corruption is everywhere in this world, though it is well hidden. Rulers have many advisors they depend on. That is how corruption starts. A trusted advisor tells the ruler a lie in an effort to create a situation to help himself or someone close to him. A ruler may lie to get a friend a contract with the government, for example, and then the friend gives the trusted advisor a kick-back payment for the favor. Other advisors see this and the fact that it was not punished. So, they too seek to enrich themselves by similar corrupt actions. Pretty soon the entire cabinet is corrupt.

13 The poor and the oppressor have this in common:
    The LORD gives sight to the eyes of both.

Proverbs 14:31 says, "Whoever oppresses the poor shows contempt for their Maker, but whoever is kind to the needy honors God."

Everyone on this earth was created by God, so we are all His people. To oppress and show contempt for the poor is oppressing and showing contempt for God's people. This is an insult to God's character and design. Being kind to the needy, on the other hand, is honoring God and all His people.

14 If a king judges the poor with fairness,
   his throne will be established forever.

A wise and fair ruler will pass fair judgments on his people regardless of whether they are rich or poor. As a result, his people will recognize the ruler's fairness and appreciate the just society they live in. The king's throne will be established as long as he treats his people fairly and does not oppress them.

15 A rod and a reprimand impart wisdom,
   but a child left undisciplined disgraces its mother.

Proverbs 13:24 says, "Whoever spares the rod hates their children, but the one who loves their children is careful to discipline them."

Proverbs 23:13-14 says, "Do not withhold discipline from a child' if you punish them with the rod, they will not die. Punish them with the rod and save them from death."

The greatest responsibility that God gives parents is to teach and guide their children. A parent striking his or her child with a rod is a metaphor for discipline. Parents discipline their children to teach them to do good and to stay off the crooked path. Discipline is not an easy thing to do, but the parent who doesn't discipline his or her child "hates" the child because the parent is allowing the child to wander down the crooked path to death and ruin.

In contrast, parents who discipline their children love them because they are teaching them to stay on the straight path that leads to righteousness, averting long-term disaster and disgrace.

> 16 When the wicked thrive, so does sin,
> but the righteous will see their downfall.

When the wicked are in leadership, sin prevails. People, families, and organizations become like their leaders, so if the leader is wicked, the people who follow them will adapt to the culture. These leaders will ultimately be brought down, however, and the righteous will prevail.

> 17 Discipline your children, and they will give you peace;
> they will bring you the delights you desire.

See Proverbs 13:24, 23:13-14, and 29:15. Parents who discipline their children teach them to be wise and to stay on the straight path. This is how they raise good children who become good adults who will give them peace and delight.

> 18 Where there is no revelation, people cast off restraint;
> but blessed is the one who heeds wisdom's instruction.

A *revelation* is a manifestation of divine will or truth. It is a message from God, given by a prophet, or a prophetic vision.

The proverbs are a revelation because they are a message from God, given from His prophet, King Solomon, son of King David. When a community has God's Word and is following it, it acts as divine guidance. When a community does not have God's Word, however, the people have no guidance and do whatever they want, usually resulting in wicked and sinful actions. Blessed are those who follow God's Word and heed wisdom's instruction.

> 19 Servants cannot be corrected by mere words;
> though they understand, they will not respond.

This verse is referring to the relationship between a servant, or slave, and his or her master. Much like children, they must be trained and instructed to free them from their rebellious hearts (known as holding people accountable in our culture today). People, or employees, need to be instructed and corrected. If they do not heed the instruction and correction, they should be punished or removed.

> 20 Do you see someone who speaks in haste?
> There is more hope for a fool than for them.

Those who speak in haste are those who blurt out the first thing that comes to their minds. This is what a fool does. Words spoken in haste can tear down people's lives, careers, and feelings.

The wise, on the other hand, give careful consideration to the words they speak. Carefully chosen, well-spoken words can calm a volatile situation or land someone a new job, contract, or spouse.

> 21 A servant pampered from youth
>   will turn out to be insolent.

Insolent means presumptuous and insulting in manner or speech, arrogant. Servants pampered from youth have received no discipline or training. They will be arrogant, rebellious in manner and speech, for which they will be dealt with as described in Proverbs 29:19.

> 22 An angry person stirs up conflict,
>   and a hot-tempered person commits many sins.

This matter is also mentioned in Proverbs 10:19, 11:12, 12:18, 15:18. Fools, the hot-tempered people, run their mouths, cause trouble, and commit many sins. The wise keep their mouths shut or speak soothing words of healing that calm a situation.

> 23 Pride brings a person low,
>   but the lowly in spirit gain honor.

Pride or arrogance will be a person's downfall. A lack of pride, or humility, which is cultivated through a fear of the Lord, will create a spirit of wisdom and honor.

> 24 The accomplices of thieves are their own enemies;
> they are put under oath and dare not testify.

An accomplice to a crime has committed a crime too. That person has walked the crooked path, approaching death and ruin. Now what? Testify so the thief and his cartel kill you for testifying against them? Or don't testify and go to jail for the crime or contempt of court? Neither are good choices. The crooked path leads to death and ruin. That's why we need to stay on the straight path.

> 25 Fear of man will prove to be a snare,
> but whoever trusts in the LORD is kept safe.

Fear of people or public opinion will hamper our ability to perform anything we try to do. The fear of the Lord is the beginning of knowledge and the foundation of wisdom. The wise do not shrink when faced with public opinion or run at the threat of persecution because they have respect, reverence, and trust in the Lord. The Lord will keep His believers safe and turn life's snares into blessings.

> 26 Many seek an audience with a ruler,
> but it is from the LORD that one gets justice.

Proverbs 29

God places our leaders and rulers in office. When they are unjust, their time is short. The Lord defends the poor and the just.

27 The righteous detest the dishonest;
   the wicked detest the upright.

This verse is the last of King Solomon's second collection. It highlights the opposing perspectives of the righteous and the wicked. They detest each other because they stand for opposite things and have a completely different set of values.

Proverbs 30

SAYINGS OF AGUR

1 The sayings of Agur son of Jakeh—an inspired utterance.
This man's utterance to Ithiel:
"I am weary, God,
but I can prevail.
2 Surely I am only a brute, not a man;
I do not have human understanding.
3 I have not learned wisdom,
nor have I attained to the knowledge of the Holy One.
4 Who has gone up to heaven and come down?
Whose hands have gathered up the wind?
Who has wrapped up the waters in a cloak?
Who has established all the ends of the earth?
What is his name, and what is the name of his son?
Surely you know!

This is a God-inspired message of a prophet, Agur, who is weary and tired in his efforts to attain the knowledge of God and wisdom, but is determined that he will never quit. In his difficult quest, however, he is expressing self-loathing and humility as he asks God very probing questions highlighting the separation between God and humanity. Many believe the verse, "Who has gone up to heaven and come down?" is a reference to Jesus Christ. This could be a prophecy written before Christ was born, which He fulfilled in the New Testament.

> 5 "Every word of God is flawless;
> he is a shield to those who take refuge in him.
> 6 Do not add to his words,
> or he will rebuke you and prove you a liar.
> 7 "Two things I ask of you, LORD;
> do not refuse me before I die:
> 8 Keep falsehood and lies far from me;
> give me neither poverty nor riches,
> but give me only my daily bread.
> 9 Otherwise, I may have too much and disown you
> and say, 'Who is the LORD?'
> Or I may become poor and steal,
> and so dishonor the name of my God.

In these verses, Agur is referencing the knowledge and wisdom of God. We can take refuge in God and His Word and be shielded from the world. God's Word is perfect, and it shall not be altered for anyone's personal

Proverbs 30

benefit. Agur is asking God for two things: 1) Do not refuse me before I die, and 2) Keep falsehood and lies far from me. His goal is to be with God in heaven when he dies, and he recognizes that being a liar could prevent that. Being extremely poor or extremely rich both have their drawbacks and cause people to pull away from God. But here the prophet is asking God for a humble life so he can honor God all his days on earth, resulting in the afterlife he wants.

> 10 "Do not slander a servant to their master,
>   or they will curse you, and you will pay for it.

Taking advantage of a servant's lowly social standing would be falsely accusing the servant to his or her master, and in turn, the servant will be punished for something he or she didn't do. The servant, however, will be justified in cursing his or her accuser for the false statement, and the accuser will pay for it. We reap what we sow.

> 11 "There are those who curse their fathers
>   and do not bless their mothers;
> 12 those who are pure in their own eyes
>   and yet are not cleansed of their filth;
> 13 those whose eyes are ever so haughty,
>   whose glances are so disdainful;
> 14 those whose teeth are swords
>   and whose jaws are set with knives
>   to devour the poor from the earth
>   and the needy from among mankind.

The fifth commandment says, "Honor your father and your mother, so that you may live long in the land the Lord your God is giving you." Failing to follow God's law could start a child down a crooked path of arrogance and pride. The wicked are intent on devouring the needy and the poor with their greed and oppression. Maybe if parents spent a little more time with their children, instructing them in wisdom and knowledge and disciplining them when necessary, the children might avoid this crooked path.

> 15 "The leech has two daughters.
> 'Give! Give!' they cry.
> "There are three things that are never satisfied,
> four that never say, 'Enough!':
> 16 the grave, the barren womb,
> land, which is never satisfied with water,
> and fire, which never says, 'Enough!'

These verses are explaining the unquenchable appetite and cravings of this world. "Three things that are never satisfied, four that never say, 'Enough!'" is a poetic way of saying the list is not complete. The leech craves blood, which they suck out from their victims. The grave yearns for the end of life. The barren womb yearns to produce life. Land yearns for water necessary to produce life, trees that produce oxygen, and crops that produce food. And fire yearns to burn, and it never says, "Enough!" to how much it has devoured.

The wise recognize that life and death are engaged in an unending battle.

> 17 "The eye that mocks a father,
>   that scorns an aged mother,
>   will be pecked out by the ravens of the valley,
>   will be eaten by the vultures.

Once again, a reference to the fifth commandment: "Honor your father and your mother, so that you may live long in the land the Lord your God is giving you."

> 18 "There are three things that are too amazing for me,
>   four that I do not understand:
> 19 the way of an eagle in the sky,
>   the way of a snake on a rock,
>   the way of a ship on the high seas,
>   and the way of a man with a young woman.

Again, "three things" or "four" is a poetic way of saying the list is not complete. The four things described truly are amazing. Watching an eagle soar in the sky. The way a snake works his way across a rock, almost effortlessly. The way a ship handles itself surviving very large waves in the ocean. And the way of a man with a young woman describes the mystery of love and the magnetic attraction that brings a man and a woman together in true love. This is equally amazing.

20 "This is the way of an adulterous woman:
   She eats and wipes her mouth
   and says, 'I've done nothing wrong.'

As described many times in Proverbs, the way of the adulterous woman is a crooked path that leads to death and ruin. She does not care who gets devoured in her wake. Eating and wiping her mouth means that she is having sexual relations with someone other than her spouse because her appetite for sex is like someone who is always hungry. She thinks nothing of it, saying "I've done nothing wrong."

21 "Under three things the earth trembles,
    under four it cannot bear up:
22 a servant who becomes king,
    a godless fool who gets plenty to eat,
23 a contemptible woman who gets married,
    and a servant who displaces her mistress.

The word *contempt* means a reproachable disdain for something vile or dishonorable, or being disgusted. The word *contemptible* means deserving of contempt, or despicable.

These verses are referring to things that can make society break down, such as people finding themselves in places they were not meant to be, and they have no training or knowledge on how to carry out the position. Examples of this are a servant becoming a king, a godless

Proverbs 30 333

fool with no wisdom who gets lucky and finds prosperity and success, an adulterous woman who gets married, or a servant who displaces her mistress.

Back in the times of Proverbs, if a wife was unable to conceive, a husband could lay with one of their servants to have children. In this instance, the servant wants to become the wife and the wife feels insecure and threatened by the servant's ability to bear children. So, the societal rules of the household completely break down.

> 24 "Four things on earth are small,
>   yet they are extremely wise:
> 25 Ants are creatures of little strength,
>   yet they store up their food in the summer;
> 26 hyraxes are creatures of little power,
>   yet they make their home in the crags;
> 27 locusts have no king,
>   yet they advance together in ranks;
> 28 a lizard can be caught with the hand,
>   yet it is found in kings' palaces.

The four creatures mentioned in these verses compensate for their small stature by their wisdom, knowledge, and work ethic. Ants work endlessly and in coordination with one another. The hyrax is an herbivorous mammal that resembles a woodchuck or a beaver, known for building shelters. Think of the massive dams with multiple rooms and underwater access that beavers build. Locusts work in unity with strict discipline to destroy whatever they have set out to eat. And lizards have the uncanny ability to get into things they're not supposed to be in. These four creatures are extremely wise. We could learn a lot by watching them use their God-given wisdom.

> 29 "There are three things that are stately in their stride,
>   four that move with stately bearing:
> 30 a lion, mighty among beasts,
>   who retreats before nothing;
> 31 a strutting rooster, a he-goat,
>   and a king secure against revolt.
> 32 "If you play the fool and exalt yourself,
>   or if you plan evil,
>   clap your hand over your mouth!
> 33 For as churning cream produces butter,
>   and as twisting the nose produces blood,
>   so stirring up anger produces strife."

These verses promote humility, respect, and social order in place of arrogance and wickedness. The lion, a strutting rooster, a he-goat, and a king are all strong leaders. Don't become arrogant in trying to exalt yourself. Putting your hand over your mouth is a euphemism for stopping what you're doing. If you don't, you're setting yourself up for a fall filled with blood and strife.

PROVERBS 31

SAYINGS OF KING LEMUEL

1 The sayings of King Lemuel—an inspired utterance his mother taught him.

Little is known about King Lemuel except that he was a king who received wise teachings from his mother. His name means "devoted to God."

2 Listen, my son! Listen, son of my womb!
  Listen, my son, the answer to my prayers!
3 Do not spend your strength on women,
  your vigor on those who ruin kings.

This mother, who is most likely a wife to a king, as well, is giving her son, who is now the king, advice. Kings in these times had great harems of wives and a large number of concubines. King Solomon had a harem of seven hundred wives. A concubine is a woman who was not the king's wife but who the king had sexual relations with and took care of. King Solomon had three hundred concubines, as well. One can imagine the physical stamina and mental strife it would take to have sexual relations with 1000 partners, help raise all the children produced, and deal with the jealousy from all the women. Women have been the downfall of many kings. The mother's advice to her son was not to waste time on self-indulgence, but to concentrate on being the best king he could be.

> 4 It is not for kings, Lemuel—
> it is not for kings to drink wine,
> not for rulers to crave beer,
> 5 lest they drink and forget what has been decreed,
> and deprive all the oppressed of their rights.
> 6 Let beer be for those who are perishing,
> wine for those who are in anguish!
> 7 Let them drink and forget their poverty
> and remember their misery no more.

Consuming too much alcohol clouds the mind, leads to blackouts, and contributes to stupid decisions. A king under the influence of alcohol would make poor decisions that deprive the oppressed of their rights. Having an intoxicated king also opens the door for someone to attempt a coup. The sick and miserable drink alcohol to forget their misery, but it is not fitting for a king.

Proverbs 31

> 8 Speak up for those who cannot speak for themselves,
> for the rights of all who are destitute.
> 9 Speak up and judge fairly;
> defend the rights of the poor and needy.

Kings are God's leaders appointed to carry out an organized and just society. A good king puts his subjects' needs and wants before his own. The same is true for all leaders today. Good leaders stick up for those who cannot stick up for themselves, speak up when they see an injustice, and do not turn their heads and just keep walking. They judge fairly and defend the rights of the underprivileged.

EPILOGUE: THE WIFE OF NOBLE CHARACTER

The proverbs have a lot to say about women. How fitting for the proverbs to end with a section on a noble wife of strong character, great wisdom, and compassion.

> 10 A wife of noble character who can find?
> She is worth far more than rubies.

A wife of noble character is indeed a rare find. This was addressed in Proverbs 11:22, so please refer back to that verse and its accompanying commentary.

> 11 Her husband has full confidence in her
> and lacks nothing of value.

The noble wife is masterful in many skills: fearing God, working hard, respecting her spouse, acquiring wisdom, handling money, farming, running a business, and many other skills. Her husband loves her and does not worry that she cannot handle her jobs. He has full confidence in her.

12 She brings him good, not harm,
    all the days of her life.

The noble wife works with her husband; they are a team. It's not "me" or "him"; it's "us." They are one unit. She makes her decisions on what is best for her husband over what is best for herself. She is completely dedicated to her husband and longs to spend her entire life with him.

13 She selects wool and flax
    and works with eager hands.

Wool and flax were made into clothing. The Proverbs 31 wife has a wise eye and selects the best material at the best price. Then she creates the clothing with her own hands and driving work ethic.

14 She is like the merchant ships,
    bringing her food from afar.

Proverbs 31

15 She gets up while it is still night;
　　she provides food for her family
　　and portions for her female servants.

The noble wife takes care of feeding her family as well as those who work for her. She awakens before dawn and works tirelessly to see that everyone gets fed at the start of their day.

16 She considers a field and buys it;
　　out of her earnings she plants a vineyard.

The Proverbs 31 wife is also an enterprising businesswoman. She buys a field to plant a vineyard with the money she earns from selling her garments and trading crops. Then she uses the vineyard as another income stream to sustain her family.

17 She sets about her work vigorously;
　　her arms are strong for her tasks.
18 She sees that her trading is profitable,
　　and her lamp does not go out at night.
19 In her hand she holds the distaff
　　and grasps the spindle with her fingers.

The noble wife is a hard worker, staying up late and rising early to achieve her tasks. As described previously, her trading is profitable in the purchase of a field for a vineyard.

20 She opens her arms to the poor
   and extends her hands to the needy.

The noble wife is compassionate and extends her hands and prosperity to the needy.

21 When it snows, she has no fear for her household;
   for all of them are clothed in scarlet.
22 She makes coverings for her bed;
   she is clothed in fine linen and purple.

The noble wife makes almost everything that her family needs: garments, coats, bed coverings. She goes the extra mile and produces fine linen in purple and scarlet.

23 Her husband is respected at the city gate,
   where he takes his seat among the elders of the land.

A husband is proud of his noble wife. Everyone knows what is going on. If someone has a wicked wife, everyone knows it and no one respects her. As the saying goes, behind every great man is a great woman.

24 She makes linen garments and sells them,
   and supplies the merchants with sashes.
25 She is clothed with strength and dignity;
   she can laugh at the days to come.

Proverbs 31

The noble wife has many skills, but is also talented in business. She and her family are secure, which gives them strength and dignity to endure troublesome days to come.

26 She speaks with wisdom,
    and faithful instruction is on her tongue.

Proverbs 1:7 says, "The fear of the Lord is the beginning of knowledge, but fools despise wisdom and instruction." The fear of the Lord is the foundation of wisdom. The noble wife has a fear of the Lord and wisdom. She shares her instruction and wisdom with her family as well as others who seek it.

27 She watches over the affairs of her household
    and does not eat the bread of idleness.

The noble wife runs her household like a well-oiled machine. "…does not eat the bread of idleness" means she is not lazy; she is always working.

28 Her children arise and call her blessed;
    her husband also, and he praises her:

The noble wife has earned the well-deserved respect of her children and her husband.

29 "Many women do noble things,
    but you surpass them all."

The noble wife goes above and beyond what is expected of the average wife. She surpasses them all and is greatly rewarded for it in family love and prosperity.

> 30 Charm is deceptive, and beauty is fleeting;
> but a woman who fears the LORD is to be praised.

Exterior beauty goes away and charm can be temporary. As referenced previously, beauty on the inside is forever. A wise and noble wife, who fears the Lord, is to be praised and cherished.

> 31 Honor her for all that her hands have done,
> and let her works bring her praise at the city gate.

The noble wife should be recognized and praised for all she has done. She has made herself and her family proud. She epitomizes the proverbs and all the instruction they have put forth.

Proverbs began with "The fear of the Lord is the beginning of knowledge, but fools despise wisdom and instruction" (verse 1:5) and ends by describing a woman who embodies all the qualities the proverbs have put forth. Wisdom and the fear of the Lord are not mere intellectual qualities; they are a way of life.

BIBLIOGRAPHY

Life Application Study Bible, NIV, Zondervan

NIV Zondervan Study Bible

NIV Study Bible, Zondervan

The Holy Bible, Harding's Superfine Edition, William D. Harding 1869

Gotquestions.org

Biblehub.com

Biblestorytools.com

Biblegateway.com

Bible.com

Openbible.info

American Heritage Dictionary, 2nd College Edition

Google.com